Vintage CHAMPAGNE
ON THE
EDGE *of* SPACE

Vintage CHAMPAGNE
ON THE
EDGE *of* SPACE

The Supersonic World of a
CONCORDE STEWARDESS

SALLY ARMSTRONG

Dedicated to JD for his inspiration
and to Rob, my son, to give him inspiration.

Any opinions expressed in this material are those of the author and
BA employees the author interviewed, and do not reflect the view of
British Airways.

Cover illustrations. Front: top: © Zimmytws/Dreamstime.com; *bottom:*
curve of the Earth © Mike Bannister; Concorde © Frederic Carmel.

First published 2015

The History Press
The Mill, Brimscombe Port
Stroud, Gloucestershire, GL5 2QG
www.thehistorypress.co.uk

© Sally Armstrong 2015

British Library Cataloguing in Publication Data.
A catalogue record for this book is available from the British Library.

ISBN 978 0 7509 6377 0

Typesetting and origination by The History Press
Printed and bound in Malta, by Melita Press

CONTENTS

ACKNOWLEDGEMENTS

I would like to give my thanks to all the crew who willingly volunteered their stories about their careers on Concorde. Certain episodes will always remain strongly etched on the mind and it is those episodes of an extraordinary life that I have happily recalled.

In particular, I would like to thank cabin service manager Dick Bell, Scarlett Geen, Louise Brown, Dee Bull, Jill Channon, Annie Carter, Carol Cornwell, Steve Brennan, Sue Drayton, Bernadette Forrest, Jeannette Hartley, Robert Bailey, Maggie Sinclair, Maggie Coles, Captain John Hutchinson, Captain Jock Lowe, Chief Pilot Mike Bannister and, last but not least, Purser Julia van den Bosch, who has flown more supersonic miles than anyone on this planet!

I would also like to thank all the crews who flew with me for all the special memories we shared. Thanks to Amy Rigg and all at The History Press for their help and support. To special friends Jilly Cooper and Fred Finn and to Richard Noble for their kind contributions to the book.

Finally, this book is not intended in any way as a technical narrative on Concorde so any omissions on its performance, handling and statistics will, I hope, be forgiven by the readers of this book.

Front cover photos – thanks to Mike Bannister and Frederic Carmel.

FOREWORD
BY RICHARD NOBLE

It's June 2009 and I am standing under the wings of Concorde Delta Golf at Brooklands. There are crowds of people around and we are here to launch the cockpit simulator which had been rescued from Filton, where it had been irreverently trashed when Concorde flying ceased. There are quite a few children present and it suddenly occurs to me that they will never see or experience Concorde fly. They must be wondering what all this is about and why they have been let down by technology and our current less-than-amazing culture.

I'm a lucky one. I was asked by British Airways (BA) to set a record for the fastest ever triple crossing of the Atlantic to celebrate ten years of Concorde transatlantic flying. We were taking G-BOAA to Kennedy (John F. Kennedy Airport, New York), and it was the same aircraft and crew who made the inaugural flight on 22 November 1977.

We are BA 001 and we leave at 10.30 a.m. to the second. I change Concordes at Kennedy, running across the tarmac to G-BOAG which is waiting for me, and by 1830 hours I am in the cockpit and on finals to Heathrow, Runway 27, when a message comes through for me, 'Richard please pick up the BA chairman's baggage on your return flight – it got left behind!'

Armed with the chairman's cases I am on my way back to Kennedy for the second time that day – and on arrival we all have a humongous party at Mortimer's in New York. The next morning I am on a Concorde flight back to London and then I am immediately off to work in our office, selling our production light aircraft to Brazil. I have absolutely no jet lag.

Including stops, the three trips took 11 hours and 22 minutes. The average speed, including stops, was 864mph.

'Do anything special over the weekend?' asks our chief designer, Bruce Giddings.

'Well, yes, I can claim to be the only person ever to have crossed the Atlantic three times in 12 hours …'

Sally Armstrong's book tells you all about the very special Concorde people who kept the service running to the very high standard that BA demands. It was a lifetime's experience to fly with them.

But there is another, even more important story. Concorde was a dramatic symbol and a source of huge pride to the British. I remember standing outside our dentist's surgery in Teddington, Middlesex, and seeing Concorde make its standard low level U-turn overhead to set off west for Kennedy. The whole street had stopped and everyone was looking up. Of course, this happened every day – and every day the Brits took enormous pride in their truly beautiful aircraft.

What Concorde did was inspire and encourage a vast number of people to become engineers, scientists and flight crew. It was a symbol of outstanding achievement by an extraordinary generation of very capable and focused people – and now their children will never see it fly. Even worse, the reality of Concorde has been replaced by singing, cooking and dancing on television and fakery in computer gaming. Concorde and its service was real. No wonder that today there is a critical shortage of engineers and scientists in our country. Could we ever do this again? I doubt it.

So, Concorde was a very special programme in a very special age. Just how special? Well, read Sally Armstrong's book – and you'll find out. I promise you won't be disappointed!

Richard Noble
Kingston upon Thames
Land-speed record holder, 1983–97

FOREWORD

BY FRED FINN

Fred Finn, the
world's most
travelled man.

When I was asked to write the foreword to this wonderful book, *Vintage Champagne on the Edge of Space*, I was thrilled to accept. I flew with Sally Armstrong on the 'Queen of the Skies' many times.

I was privileged to belong to the Concorde group of friends. With 718 flights in Concorde, I got to know the wonderful cabin crew very well during a thirty-year love affair with this extraordinary, beautiful and graceful lady of the skies. As a result we became good friends – there was always a chilled bottle of DP [Dom Perignon] shampoo under the seat in front when I boarded into my seat, 9a.

There were occasions when I was asked to give my seat to someone they didn't want to leave behind. On those occasions I used to sit in the jump seat behind the captain, most of whom I got to know socially, having played cricket for the Concorde cricket team in the annual match in Allworth village at the local pub. It was the home of the first captain, Brian Calvert, who organised the very first Concorde charter with the gamekeeper and the poacher on board.

Concorde was the only aircraft that had this friendly, fun and yet extremely professional atmosphere, where it appeared that everyone knew the regulars and, in my case, I was known as Fred. I used to look forward to being on board and, of course, it was quicker than a rifle bullet. I got so used to the atmosphere on Concorde flights that I began to think the flights were too quick. I didn't ever want this part of my life and world ever to stop.

Thank you to my many Concorde crew friends, some of whom I still see and continue to enjoy that special relationship that only Concorde could have created, and to Sally for this real account of life on Concorde.

Where else could you have John Denver playing 'Country Road', Paul McCartney drawing happy faces, and the 'boss' Bruce Springsteen asking 'how many flights for Fred now?' to the crew?

Concorde, and my friends on Concorde, I miss you – it was a disaster that it was pulled out of the skies so prematurely, nothing else comes close. It was so much, much more than just an aircraft. The aircraft lived and breathed – Concorde was alive.

The world has gone back to those ubiquitous bi-bodied impersonal sons of Boeing and Airbus, a retroactive step. Nothing will ever be the same again in the world of aviation.

Fred Finn
718 flights in Concorde, 16 million miles –
Guinness World Records held since 1983
Director of Livingstone's Travel World
Co-founder of 'Quicket', the mobile travel app
President of Save Concorde Group

Sally Armstrong.

INTRODUCTION

She's fast, she's slinky and the captain loves her.

So ran the headline in a newspaper. This was not some story about a captain's love affair with a stewardess, this was not some insider's 'tell all' story about a romance in the flying world – this was the description of a unique aircraft. This was about Concorde.

There are not many aircraft in aviation history that can match the description, or earn the love and devotion from the many hundreds who worked on her, both on the ground and in the air. Concorde, with her unique elegant silhouette, was impossible to ignore as she streamed across the skies. To compare her to a very beautiful woman is easy. She was the ultimate head turner. She had a beautifully designed body, she was elegant and, like a beautiful woman, never failed to cause a stir of attention.

For the captains and flight crew 'going to work' was always a joy. Flying your own 'dream machine' that had cost zillions was not a bad way to earn a living and most pilots will confess to that. For the cabin crew it was the ultimate in flying as a career.

For the passengers it invariably stirred a childhood excitement. Flying on the outer edge of space never failed to impress even the most regular passengers. It was exhilarating. It was unlike any other passenger aircraft in aviation history. Even after its twenty-seven years' service it was still an icon. Here is my story of Concorde, the ultimate flying machine.

Sally Armstrong

THE END OF AN ERA –
TEARS AND CHEERS:
LONDON HEATHROW AIRPORT

On 24 October 2003, the world's press, TV camera crews and many thousands of spectators gathered at London's Heathrow Airport. Every available spot around the perimeter roads was crammed with devoted fans. Police cordons were set up to ensure the spectators kept to their side of the barriers. A grandstand had been specially erected to hold 1,000 people.

Contrary to most VIP arrivals it wasn't the guest list on board the incoming aircraft that was the subject of their attention. It wasn't the arrival of a mega pop star who fans waited excitedly to see. It was the *actual* aircraft that held their focus of attention. But this was no ordinary arrival and no ordinary landing. A momentous event was about to happen. The landing of this iconic aircraft would herald the end of an era of supersonic flying.

It was Concorde the world waited for. This aviation phenomenon of the twentieth and twenty-first centuries was making its final commercial flight into London's Heathrow Airport. At the exact appointed time and, like a diva making her appearance right on cue on the world's stage, the distinctive shape of Concorde appeared through the clouds, its pointed drooping nose leading the swanlike contours of its wing structure. Elegant and graceful, its four Rolls-Royce Olympus 593 engines throttled back as it made its final approach.

The spectators held their breath, marvelling for the last time at Concorde's timeless elegance. History was being made, and this was one piece of history the public wanted to be a part of. Concorde was very close to their hearts and, in a time of economic uncertainty and upheavals in politics, it gave them a reason to be proud of being British. Concorde fans had come in their thousands to pay their last respects. Many millions more around the world watched on TV.

As Concorde approached Heathrow Airport for the last time in its twenty-seven years of commercial history, few could take in this moment. It was incomprehensible that the familiar shape that passed overhead on its 'regular as clockwork' arrival time into Heathrow would be, from this day, missing from our skies – that we would never again witness its feminine, graceful contours as it accelerated away to its supersonic altitude.

Concorde was to be consigned to the history books. Could we believe that the fastest passenger aircraft ever, able to cross the Atlantic in the same time it takes a train to get from London to Manchester, would now be ignominiously fated to sit in a hangar, never to fly the skies again?

The world was witnessing the end of an era, and the British public along with all the workers who been a part of its history were mourning its fate. Concorde had been the miracle of the twentieth and twenty-first centuries.

The first Concorde (G-BOAE) landed at 4.01 p.m. from Edinburgh. This flight had left London in the morning. Many of its passengers for the return flight were British Airways (BA) staff who had been lucky enough to win standby tickets in a prize draw. They had flown from London to Edinburgh subsonic. In the Executive Lounge at Edinburgh Airport they had enjoyed a champagne style reception as they watched Concorde land to the sound of bagpipes and cheering crowds. Amongst the passengers was a group of British Airways cabin crew. They felt very sorry for the working crew who, as one said, 'were very emotional. The crew hold Concorde very dear to their hearts.' As they took off it wasn't only the crew who were feeling the weight of the moment. For the passengers on board, the emotionally charged atmosphere must have been an ironic mix of a party and a funeral wake.

The second Concorde (G-BOAF), having completed a supersonic flight around the Bay of Biscay, followed at 4.03 p.m. Three minutes later, the final Concorde (G-BOAG), flight BA 002, landed from New York. This Concorde had departed from London the evening before. Its passengers, who were avid enthusiasts, had paid £9,000 for a ticket.

Concorde had experienced a wonderful send-off in New York, its departure commemorated by a water canon spray of blue, red and white to evoke the colours of Great Britain, France and America. As flight BA 002 made its final approach into Heathrow with all the grace and finesse of the great ballerina Darcy Bussell (who was herself on that flight), the event was, without doubt, a tear-jerking moment.

Few who witnessed the sight of Concorde's final landing will forget the poignancy as Captain Mike Bannister taxied the aircraft and dipped Concorde's nose in salute to the crowds, waving the Union Jack from out of the cockpit window. The air traffic controllers responded with the message, 'The eagles have landed – welcome home.'

Chief Pilot Captain Bannister, who had joined the Concorde fleet in 1977 as its youngest pilot, commented that they had tried to make the day of Concorde's retirement a celebration that both the public and airline could look back on with pride.

Flight 002 was a celebrity packed flight. Luminaries such as the BA chairman, Lord Marshall, Sir David Frost, the Duke of Kent and Sir Andrew Lloyd Webber were on board. Sir Terence Conran, who two years earlier had redesigned the Concorde interior, was a guest along with Julien Macdonald, designer of the new BA uniforms. Actress Joan Collins and her husband, Percy Gibson, Jeremy Clarkson, politician Tony Benn and Bernie Ecclestone were all on the VIP passenger list.

Purser Julia van den Bosch is the longest serving Concorde stewardess. She joined it in 1976 and was on this last flight from New York. She shares her memories of the last flight:

We were all very aware that we were making history. When we arrived in New York the day before our last flight home, we sat down in the hotel and did a lot of signing of memorabilia and autographs and gave interviews. I had also given a lot of interviews in London before Concorde's departure as the interest was global – journalists had arrived from all over the world. Before I left London, friends and neighbours were coming to my door asking me if I would take something belonging to them on the flight with me just so they could say it had been on Concorde's last flight. They felt that strongly about it.

In New York we signed first day covers, flight certificates and gave each other mementos. We had the British Airways wine and food supervisors come to tell us exactly what we would be serving for the flight home and we went through the meal schedule. The evening concluded with a wonderful last night dinner at La Cirque.

The really strange thing was that British Airways would not allow the occasion to be written up as 'sad' and kept insisting that the last flight was a 'celebration' of Concorde, and we were all briefed accordingly. Of course the press spent the whole time trying to catch photos of us crying to prove the airline wrong!

None of us could feel that it was a celebration. It was an incredibly sad occasion, but equally we wanted to do our best. In one interview with the BBC I said that I wanted to say thank you to Concorde, because it had been quite some journey and I had done such wonderful things in my time with her. Likewise with the passengers, I think they all were very aware of the historical significance of the flight – especially as we had people on board who had been hugely connected with the aircraft right from the beginning.

The flight itself was chaotic – our cabin had all the press, two of whom, Mary Nightingale and Jeremy Bowen, were broadcasting live, and those who weren't broadcasting live were trying to interview the celebs, so it was 'Oh I'll eat later', or 'leave it over there would you and I'll get round to it' – so I said to the crew, 'We have to say no. There is no later, it's now or never! And on this flight, we really mean it's now or never!'

For all the crews who had worked on Concorde, the engineers, ground crew, pilots and cabin crew, it was the break-up of a close-knit family. The Concorde crews and staff were an elite group who never lost sight of the privilege of working on such a special aircraft. To fly Concorde was an unrivalled aviation experience.

To work on it was to be a part of a special team and at the forefront of the British Airways flagship. For the flight crew it meant keeping to the tight arrival and departure schedules. For the engineers it meant keeping Concorde up to its mechanical best and for the ground crew, to ensure the passengers check-in ran like clockwork. The cabin crew had to be at their most professional, with a service that was second to none, and the five-course meal served during the constrained flight time had to be as near perfect as possible, given the size of the supersonic restaurant and its 100 guests.

It must have been a supremely difficult decision for British Airways management to pull the plug on their flagship aircraft and many believe it was indeed a step backwards for mankind. Who can honestly say they never stopped to stand and stare as it flew overhead? Concorde never became mundane. Its familiarity in the skies never bred indifference. If it was still flying today I'm sure the same would be true. As it cruised over London just after 1800 hours, at the start of its Atlantic journey, and then the return flight from New York coming over just before 2200 hours, its unique engine noise never let one forget that overhead was an exotic and glamorous icon.

Another great British icon was Frankel, the nation's favourite racehorse. He had bowed out of his spectacular racing career and experienced a similar exit on his retirement in 2012. Thousands of fans and ardent racegoers turned out to watch him at Ascot in his last ever race. It made headlines across the world. It was a sad day to see such a fine horse being retired to a stud farm. Frankel was a true thoroughbred and unbeaten in his race history. In the case of Concorde, however, there was no future generation to carry on the marvels of supersonic flight.

With her exceptional flying ability, Concorde was often described as a thoroughbred by the men and women who flew her. Jock Lowe, the longest serving pilot on the Concorde fleet and former president of the Royal Aeronautical Society, elucidates on this. He describes her as being more advanced than the Apollo 11 that put the first men on the moon and, in terms of manoeuvrability and power, she was on a par with or even better than any military aircraft of the time.

As a member of the Concorde cabin crew and flying supersonic at 60,000ft, it was for me another day of 'going to the office', and in this case going to the office was always a consummate adventure.

CONCORDE BEGINNINGS AND DESIGN ISSUES

The development of Concorde is a wonderfully intriguing story in itself. It was as early as 1956 that a British project was started with the view to developing a supersonic passenger aircraft, and two years later it had been agreed by the Supersonic Transport Advisory Committee that it was indeed a feasible project.

In 1962 the British and French governments signed an agreement for joint design, development and manufacture of a supersonic airliner. A workforce of over 200,000 were engaged on the project, which incidentally was on the same scale as the American space programme to the moon. Ten years later, British Overseas Airways Corporation (BOAC) ordered five Concorde into production and Air France ordered four.

To get her to the stage of commercial operation there was, naturally, a huge amount of costly development and many obstacles to overcome and there is no question that flying ordinary men at an altitude of 60,000ft without space suits was one of the greatest technological achievements of the age. The intricacies of design and development were such amazing achievements for the time that it could be described as the new Elizabethan age in aircraft development. They are deserving of a book in themselves, of which there have been many superb ones written by the pilots.

However, some of the design development cannot be passed by without a mention. The simple, yet elegant shape of Concorde with the swept-back delta wing was unique to a passenger aircraft. Although efficient in supersonic flight, it was not brilliant at giving the aircraft the lift needed to propel it into the skies. Simple paper aeroplanes were used to test the wing shapes. This simple form of testing was revealed years later when papier mâché prototypes were uncovered in a dusty warehouse. These simple experiments graduated to wood then metal versions.

The Concorde wing has the appearance of total simplicity, but this was one area on the development side that took more attention than any other – 5,000 hours of testing was conducted in the wind tunnel. Looking at the delta-shaped wing head-on to the aircraft, the wing can be seen to twist and droop. As aircraft speeds have increased over time, the amount of 'sweepback' that can be seen on the wings has also increased. On traditional aircraft, the vortex (swirling air needed to give the aircraft lift) is formed on the wing tip. These can be seen on a damp day as an aircraft comes into land or take off. Trails of vapour are seen on the wing tips.

However, on Concorde's delta wing, because of the higher angle of attack on take-off (most subsonic jets leave the runway at an angle of 3–4 degrees and Concorde's angle of lift was 10–11 degrees), the vortices are formed along the entire wing tip. Thus, the end result of all the development was that the supersonic aircraft could fly at a complete range of speed, from the take-off speed, to fly gracefully at Mach 2 and then slowing down on her approach for landing.

Another massive challenge facing the designers of this innovative passenger aircraft was the issue over the air intakes. No jet engine can accept air into its compressors at supersonic speed. Necessarily the air had to be slowed by 1,000mph, from Mach 2 to Mach 0.5, in order to enter the engines. The British engineers achieved a feat that had never been done before with computers that technically were not in common use at the time. These computers controlled the flow of air into the engine via hydraulically powered ramps that moved up and down to control the airflow and reduce its speed.

A view inside Concorde's cockpit. (Courtesy of Louise Brown)

To power her 180 tons into the air were four Rolls-Royce Olympus engines with massive thrust – 38,000lb, or in layman's speak, the equivalent of 3,000 family saloon cars. The power was accelerated by reheats or afterburners, a device used by fighter jets. Seen as a spectacular red glow of flame on take-off they also came with a bucketful of decibels. Take-off, from inside Concorde and watching from the ground, was nothing if not spectacular.

The take-off speed for most passenger jets varies between 160 and 180mph (260 and 290km/h). Concorde's was much faster at 225mph (360km/h) and from standstill to full take-off speed took 30 seconds. And that was 30 seconds of thrill seeking for those on board. Not only because of the speed but also the angle of climb.

Another design feature that had to be addressed was the visibility issue in the cockpit during take-off and landing. This led to the drooping nose design. By lowering it 5 degrees during taxi and take-off, and 12 degrees during landing, the pilot could have a clear view of the runway. After landing this was raised to prevent damage to the nose. After take-off the nose, along with a moving visor, was raised to improve its aerodynamic performance.

Concorde had carbon fibre brakes which back in the 1960s was a technological marvel, along with the fly-by-wire system which belonged to a new age of flying. This system replaced the heavy manual flight controls with an electronic interface so that commands from computers stabilised the aircraft.

Once the cruising speed of 1,350mph was reached, there was an issue with the outside temperature of the fuselage. Concorde's speed created friction that, in turn, created heat. The nose at this stage was hot: 127°C (261°F) to be precise.

Concorde grew 8–10in while in flight and the flight engineer's cap that was placed there during the last flight is now a permanent fixture. (Courtesy of Mike Bannister)

The rear of the aircraft was slightly cooler at 100°C (212°F). This was another developmental problem that set it apart from the subsonic commercial aircraft. A special aluminium alloy had to be developed to withstand these temperatures. Also, the visor was designed to be used as a heat shield and to deflect the heat from the cockpit. Because of this heating issue with the outside skin it also meant that the British Airways logo had to be minimal and the majority of the skin painted in highly reflective white paint to deflect the heat.

This friction and heat also caused the aircraft to expand during supersonic cruise. Concorde could grow in length by up to 300mm (1ft). This expansion was evident in the flight deck next to the engineer's console and the bulkhead adjoining it. During flight the gap made a good perch for the engineer's cap. But, of course, he had to remember to remove it before the aircraft reduced height and speed, otherwise it would have been its compulsory resting place until the aircraft flew supersonic again!

NOW, WHAT SHALL WE CALL IT? NAMING ISSUES

Finally, there was an issue with the naming of this technological marvel. This, you would have thought, would have been the easiest part of the whole story. Compare it to building a house. After years and years of planning, design and building, then comes the easy bit – giving it a name. The naming of the house is the final piece of tinsel on the Christmas tree. Deciding on a name for Concorde after years of hardcore development should have been easy, but when it came down to a French–English co-production sadly this was not so. It created tension between the French and British governments at the time.

The word '*concorde*' comes from the French word meaning harmony/agreement/union. In English we have the same word but without the 'e'. As it turned out, none of those meanings applied to the final naming of the aircraft. There was disharmony, there was disagreement, there was division and bickering that only politicians could create when it came to Anglo-French relations.

Initially, it was agreed Concorde was to be spelt with an 'e'. Then, Prime Minister Harold Macmillan decided to drop the 'e'. However, in 1967 when Concorde was finally presented to the world in Toulouse, Tony Benn, Minister for Technology, suddenly announced that Concorde would have the 'e', thereby avoiding another fracas with the French.

One would have thought that would have been the end of the 'e' story, but no – apparently there was a nationalist uproar, which only died down when Benn calmed the protesting masses by saying that the 'e' on the end of Concorde stood for 'excellence', 'England', 'Europe' and '*entente (cordiale)*'!

As if this wasn't enough, some Scotsman with a bee in his bonnet wrote to Mr Benn and informed him that part of the aircraft had been made in Scotland (the nose cone to be exact). Another civil war was averted when Mr Benn explained that 'e' (well-used by now) also stood for '*Ecosse*' (the French word for Scotland).

And the final 'e' story. In ecclesiastical terms, there is the definitive statement that even God loved Concorde. The prayer goes, 'O God who art the author of peace and lover of concord' (and not an 'e' in sight!).

As Tony Benn pointed out, Concorde came into being at a very bad time for the economy when oil prices were high and there were moves afoot to cancel Concorde production. However, with 200,000 jobs now at stake in its construction, it would have been an unwise manoeuvre to follow the Treasury's policy to scrap the project.

Tony Benn recalls one of the Concorde test flights where he sat behind the pilot wearing a parachute. Having been an RAF pilot he was quite happy to do this, although he never quite understood what use it would have been.

After the French President George Pompidou had agreed to keep Concorde, Tony Benn invited all the employees on a flight around the Bay of Biscay in the summer of 1974:

> Many of them had been working on aircraft for twenty to thirty years but many of them had never flown, and so a few were quite nervous. We went all over the Bay of Biscay, and we'd all brought sandwiches and Thermos flasks. It was like a charabanc trip to the seaside.

(By kind permission of the *Guardian* newspaper,
17 October 2003)

THE STAGE IS SET AND A NEW ICON IS BORN

When Concorde was revealed to the world in Toulouse in 1967, Brian Calvert, a very influential figure in the development of Concorde and one of a small group of BOAC captains involved in the task of preparing Concorde for service, describes vividly the day he saw the prototype for the first time. In his book *Flying Concorde* he says:

> It was a bitterly cold December day. A tiered stand with a thousand guests faced the hangar whose closed doors hid the first prototype. The hangar doors rolled back accompanied by the usual warning whistles ... and there she was, sideways on, long sharp and sleek. The shuffling and foot stamping died out, and a long silence followed as the crowd took it all in. As Concorde was towed out slowly in a wide arc we saw for the first time how the extraordinary shape seemed to change as different angles were presented. There had been photographs of course but this, the first sight of a real Concorde, stopped the breath.
>
> (By kind permission of Airlife Publishing, an imprint of The Crowood Press Ltd)

Two years later, Concorde's chief test pilot, Brian Trubshaw, took Concorde 002 on its maiden flight from Filton. Concorde prototype 001 flew supersonic for the first time on 1 October 1969 for nine minutes.

Brian Trubshaw and Brian Calvert, along with many others who were involved with the early proving flights, were indeed brave men. They were testing the unknown. Only military jets and a select group of young, fit, military pilots in pressure suits had done anything similar. Never before had men flown so close to space in an aircraft designed for commercial use. (It is interesting to note that during the test flights the pilots wore parachutes and an escape hatch had been built in the floor of the prototype Concorde in case of a potential disaster.)

It was not until 1972, five years after its initial unveiling in Toulouse, that the first orders for Concorde were taken. At the time it appeared that the whole of the aviation industry wanted to buy into supersonic flight. Options for orders were placed by many of the American airlines, notably TWA and Pan American. Iran Air, Air India, China, Qantas, Air Canada, Japanese Airlines (JAL), Lufthansa and Sabena all showed interest. A total of sixteen airlines placed options for seventy-four Concordes.

In a televised speech, President John F. Kennedy had spoken proudly of his dream of America having its own supersonic passenger aircraft, and a project – the Boeing SST – was started. The dream, however, was shelved when the true costs of development were revealed. The financial clout of Wall Street preferred money-making schemes to the massive development costs on a project that was still in doubt. They opted instead for the development of the jumbo jet. And so, in 1973, on the day the options were due to run out, both TWA and Pan American pulled the plug on Concorde. The other countries followed suit like a falling pack of cards.

Russia had been keen to join the 'supersonic club' with its own transport. It developed the prototype TU144, dubbed 'Concordski' by the British press, but its development was seriously jeopardised when it crashed spectacularly at the Paris Air Show in 1973.

It was left to the diminutive island of Great Britain and its neighbour, France, to pursue the global dream despite the escalating costs that were, by 1973, breathtakingly over budget. Had both of these governments decided to abandon the supersonic project, it is a daunting thought that Concorde may *never* have taken to the skies as a commercial concern and the world would have lost one of the greatest achievements ever.

In 1962 the total bill was expected to be between £150 million and £170 million. In 1974 this was revised to a cost of £974 million to France and Britain. The three main factors given for this sixfold increase were inflation, currency devaluation and design changes. However, as it was pointed out to the disgruntled taxpayer who effectively owned the aircraft, to have got the sums right would have been a superhuman achievement. The designers and engineers on the project were doing something that had never been done before with a commercial aircraft. They could not have known what frontiers they were pushing in this breakthrough for the aerospace industry.

And the spin-off to all this development and cost? The advancement in so many sectors of industry has been hugely influenced, from the use of computers in design and product applications, to new types of machine tools and the technology of paints, glass, plastics and non-ferrous material – all because of Concorde. Great Britain and France led the world in this new technology. Looking back to those nerve-racking days of its early development, there cannot be many who are not justly proud that this scheme evolved into making Britain a nation proud of its achievements.

THE AMERICAN RESPONSE

It was on 21 January 1976 that Concorde BA 300 began its first commercial service from Heathrow. Captain Brian Calvert, Captain Norman Todd and Engineer John Liddiard had the honour of flying this inaugural flight to Bahrain. The planning and preparation had taken many months and the world eagerly anticipated this new dawn of a supersonic era.

Among the passengers were a mixture of fare payers. Lord and Lady Leathers had taken the precaution of booking twelve years earlier. Invited guests included the Duke of Kent and senior politicians. The world's press were also on board to film and broadcast the flight.

Simultaneously, at the Charles de Gaulle Airport in Paris, an Air France Concorde was also preparing for its inaugural flight to Rio de Janeiro via Dakar. It was another landmark in Concorde's history when the two aircraft took off at precisely the same time, and it was estimated that worldwide 250 million people watched this moment.

However, Concorde's position as 'Queen of the Skies' was not unanimously received around the world. In Sydney it had arrived to an unwelcome reception by anti-noise and environmental lobbyists. In America, there were plenty of objectors, including an environmentalist group called 'the Citizens League Against the Sonic Boom'. In the *New York Times* a full-page advert appeared:

SST (Super Sonic Transport) AIRPLANE OF TOMORROW BREAKS WINDOWS, CRACKS WALLS, STAMPEDES CATTLE AND WILL HASTEN THE END OF THE AMERICAN WILDERNESS.

New York fought hard to prevent the arrival of the new noisy aircraft. Some regarded this as a sulky gesture from the USA who led the aviation industry but had not achieved their own supersonic transport. On 2 December 1970 the US Senate banned Concorde on environmental grounds.

Slowly, acceptance of Concorde was won in spite of its American antagonists. Its first appearance in the United States was to Dallas/Fort Worth Airport in September 1973 to celebrate the dedication of the new airport. It was greeted enthusiastically. By the end of 1974 Concorde had made appearances at Boston, Miami, Los Angeles, San Francisco and Anchorage, and its arrival proved to be an overall success. In Los Angeles, an estimated 250,000 turned out to see it.

Special permission by the US Secretary of Transportation was finally given for a regular service into Washington's Dulles International Airport and on 24 May 1976 both Air France and BOAC commenced their services. Before landing, both aircraft simultaneously flew over the US capital and then made parallel approaches to Dulles Airport. They touched down together and landed to a rapturous welcome. The two Concordes parked nose to nose in front of the control tower. This became a regular route and between 1984 and 1991 the route was extended to Miami via Washington three times a week.

However, Concorde's viability depended on the New York to London route. In October 1977 two Concordes (one Air France) flew to New York for a test flight to monitor the engine noise on take-off. Captain Walpole and his crew were met by a hostile press reception but he and his team had worked long and hard to find a way to reduce the noise levels. As they took off with a 25° angle of bank and a throttling back of the engines, the noise monitors hardly registered. Concorde's future was saved. Its route to New York was passed.

In less than a month its first commercial service landed at New York's John F. Kennedy Airport. However, the objectors persisted in making their views known and the crew were a target. As they left the terminal heading for the city, the protesters would bang on their coach and were vociferous in their anti-Concorde remarks. It must have felt quite ironic to the crews who were hailed as pioneers of twentieth-century travel and lauded in their own and other countries, yet were made to feel like criminals by a minority in a country that was so advanced compared to the rest of the world.

But enough of the technical metamorphosis of this aircraft. It's time to switch to the more human side of the story and how the author came to fly on Concorde.

THE AIR STEWARDESS:
HOW IT ALL BEGAN

My first memories of aeroplanes were as a child lying on the grass in my garden at home and watching the occasional jet airliner pass high overhead, its vapour trails striating a blue sky in dramatic white pastels. Like many children with time on their hands and left to their own dreams and imaginations, I would reflect on the unobtainable. In my childhood, flying was not the commonplace means of transport for taking the family to foreign destinations on holiday. Holidays were spent at home or, for the more adventurous, via an interminably long car journey to distant places like Devon or Cornwall.

Flying was what dreams were made of and as I gazed up at this world so very far from my own it left me wondering. How many passengers were inside the tiny metal tube racing across the sky? Where were they going? What was happening inside the aircraft at that moment? And how lucky were those glamorous stewardesses to be up there flying to exotic places! They were handpicked, and the consummate image of glamour and mystique. The perception of a stewardess as a tall, thin and beautiful girl was a reality then and not just in the imagination of a public relations executive. Some air hostesses, as they were then called, came from the cream of society – ex-debutantes with a spare year on their hands joined an airline to see the world. Flying was a prestigious job and with it came a suitcase full of glamour. It wasn't until Concorde landed on our horizons that this old-fashioned concept was to return.

The exotic dream of getting airborne, however, was different in reality, with my first passenger flight at the age of 17. It was not filled with the wonderment I had anticipated. Flying for the first time and alone, it was a case of nerves supplanting any idea of romance. But it did enable me to leave behind a rain-soaked English summer and transported me to the south of France to start my first foreign holiday job teaching sailing to French holidaymakers.

Several years later, having chosen my vocation as a teacher, I was flat sharing with a BOAC stewardess in Richmond, Surrey. Dutifully, and happily I might add, I would catch the bus to East Sheen Primary School every day and life became a satisfactory routine of teaching small children, amongst other things, the necessary social skills of toilet training, keeping lunch where it was designed to be once eaten (in the stomach and not thrown up in the classroom) and advising them on the uses of a handkerchief – green runny noses were not an attractive sight to anyone, least of all their squeamish teacher.

Returning home on a dank and dark winter's afternoon, having been enclosed in a germ-breeding capsule for the common cold with thirty-two infants, I was greeted by the most enormous bowl of exotic fruits on the living room coffee table. Perched mountainously high were avocados, pineapples, mangoes and peaches, all freshly flown in from Nairobi market that morning. In a vase was a towering arrangement of orange and crimson Bird of Paradise flowers. A winter's living room had, in an instant, been transformed into a luxurious haven that smelt of a tropical paradise. To bring further exotica into the picture, my very beautiful flat mate, a public relations man's dream, wafted into the room looking exceptionally healthy and with a suntan the colour of burnt toffee. The last straw was seeing her line of pretty bikinis drying above the bathroom radiator. Her 'work' for that week had been a three-day trip to Nairobi staying at the

Hilton Hotel, sunbathing by the pool along with shopping trips to the market and eating very healthily. And she got handsomely paid for all this.

As much as I loved teaching I was easily persuaded that, at the age of 22, the world was my oyster and that there were more exciting ways of earning a living, together with acquiring a midwinter suntan and the opportunity for foreign travel, such as had been the dreams of my childhood.

The prerequisites for a stewardess were slightly different then to what they are now. In the sixties and seventies, the stewardesses stayed in the job for probably no more than a year to eighteen months. It was a way to see the world, but not a chosen career as such. Many of the privately educated girls used flying as a sort of finishing school. Working as a stewardess was then still in its glamour phase and there was an aura of mystery surrounding the life. None of the girls were allowed to be married, so it was a tough choice – marry the man or lose the job. There were several girls, however, who would slip the ring off their finger before a flight hoping to get away with their 'crime' of being married. The company obviously deemed that by the age of 35 all stewardesses were past their 'fly by date'. That was the retirement age, or after ten years of service, whichever came first. Emancipation of women still had a long way to go even then …

Previous careers in teaching or nursing helped enormously when trying to get through the interview stage. A good pair of legs was also a bonus and a slim build and attractive looks were no doubt taken into account. And of course there was the smile. This was the one essential that came with the job and was used to great advantage in times of stress situations on the aircraft and for calming awkward passengers. Also required was a coolness of character in times of the odd emergency and potentially catastrophic situation (an engine fire and no landing gear could not be ruled out).

Despite the tension and nerve-racking wait for the job confirmation letter to drop through the letter box, my fairy godmother came to my assistance with my new career plans. Later that year, after two interviews and six weeks of training for 747s, I too was flying the skies proudly in my BOAC uniform.

A FLYING START – THE 747 FLEET

The 747 fleet had been in operation for four years when I joined the airline and in this year, 1974, BEA (British European Airways or 'Back Every Afternoon') had merged with BOAC (long-haul routes) to form British Airways. The first 747 commercial flight had taken place from New York to London in January 1970, but what was so remarkable was that this innovative and huge engineering feat had taken a mere twenty-eight months to design.

Like most sceptics of the time and before I started flying, I doubted that a plane of that size could actually get airborne. It appeared to defy the laws of gravity as it lumbered down the runway for what seemed like forever. Just as the last landing strip of lights appeared, the nose would lift and slowly the big beast would start to climb. There was always that doubt in my mind that it would not quite make it.

This was brought home to me quite vividly when, in the early days of my flying career on the 747, we left New York one wild, stormy night with a fifth engine on the wing. This had to be repositioned back to London and obviously the aircraft was designed to carry the extra load. However, we all doubted the idea at the time. We had a full aircraft of 430 passengers and it was a nail-biting moment on take-off. The 747 seemed to take forever to leave the runway ('Are we going by road?' one passenger asked). The captain and his flight crew made no secret of the fact that they had white knuckles during the take-off as the conditions were not ideal to get the heavyweight into the air.

The ease of working on such a spacious aircraft was wonderful. The wide aisles and galleys allowed the crew plenty of working space. With a cabin crew of thirteen plus three flight crew, the longer trips that could extend to twenty-one days were epic. Trips down through the Middle East, India, Singapore, Hong Kong, Melbourne, Sydney and Auckland were interesting in many respects. Sightseeing was always part of the itinerary if we had the time during a stopover.

Invariably the crew got on well, and more often than not the trips were a non-stop party. The job description of cabin crew then was often recalled as 'flying from party to party in an aluminium tube'. The crew 'post flight' party was virtually compulsory whatever time of night or day we landed. Even if we arrived at some unearthly early hour of the morning it was expected that all crew would meet for drinks in someone's room. It was a tough call at times, when all I wanted was for my head to hit the pillow, but, arriving at the designated room, an alcoholic drink would be put in my hand 'to help the jet lag', and a casual 'debrief' of the flight followed. Plans for the remaining stopover time were also made.

Some of these parties would warrant several chapters on their own, especially if the crew got on well and were 'party animals'. Affairs between the crew happened whichever location we happened to be in. Beautiful places like Mauritius and the Caribbean naturally lent themselves more for these to develop, with night beach parties making it hard sometimes to resist 'the romance of the moment'.

However, most crew, particularly the married ones, were very philosophical about these arrangements and the 'affairs' generally finished once the crew landed back at Heathrow. In those days the reporting office where we checked out after a flight was named 221. Aptly, there were many '221 divorces'. It was at times very difficult to adjust to coming home to the realities of life after an intense few weeks away, working hard and partying hard and in great company every day and night. There are few jobs where the workplace is so varied or the work colleagues spend so much time together. We were spending most of our time working and relaxing together and great friendships were formed.

We were entertained royally by generous hosts in the countries we visited. There were the infamous sheik's parties in Bahrain hosted by the ruler himself at his beach house, there were High Commission lunches in Delhi, party invitations to the Hong Kong Yacht Club, invitations to go to cocktail parties on board cruise liners in Bermuda, opportunities to go sailing in Sydney, Barbados and many other exotic locations. It was a privileged world.

I understand life with the airline is different now. The crews lead a far healthier lifestyle, drinking less and not socialising as much. The crew allowances, which for us were more than generous, meant that we wined and dined in style whilst away. With the downturn in the airline economy, the basic pay for cabin crew has been much reduced and so, wisely enough, the crews save their allowances and probably have much healthier livers for it!

After forty-four years the 747s have not yet been retired and are still the reliable 'workhorse' for many airlines. At any one time there are 100,000 people flying in 747s somewhere in the skies.

SUBSONIC TO SUPERSONIC

After seven years of flying the world on 747s and the body clock getting more confused by the day with jet lag, I decided it was time for a change. Flying to different parts of the globe was fine, but when the crew schedule takes you westwards to Anchorage and Osaka, Japan, and then east via India to Hong Kong, followed by yet another swing of the body clock pendulum to Los Angeles, there comes a time when the sleep routine becomes totally disrupted. The time changes were enormous.

Added to that and not helping the jet lag was my 'other' life of flying to the Grand Prix circuits in various parts of the globe with a Formula One team. I had also suffered health problems having succumbed to two bouts of salmonella in two years. The immune system had worn down somewhat and my stamina was not what it used to be. All these factors were pushing me to a more routine lifestyle – if 'flying' can in any way be mentioned in the same breath as 'routine'. My next month's schedule was to include a trip to Bombay, interesting in its myriad of cultures and lifestyles, Johannesburg, a city living on its nerves, and finally Anchorage and Osaka.

Alaska and Japan were both favourite destinations for the crew despite the huge time change. Anchorage, one of the most northern cities on the planet, was in those days little more than a one-horse town where reindeer roamed the garden suburbs, and crew trips to the spectacular mountain glaciers were always a bonus. The country around was wild and beautiful and earthquake tremors were commonplace. Biplanes taking off and landing on the great stretches of water around Anchorage were common forms of transport for the locals.

The next sector to Osaka was, again, a very extraordinary culture and it never failed to fascinate. Eating out at night was a case of choosing our dishes from the plastic replicas in the windows of the restaurants. Shopping was a new experience, too. As the stores opened their doors at exactly the appointed hour, the staff would line up inside the foyer entrance to greet their customers. A Japanese member of staff stood at the bottom of every escalator with a cloth in her gloved hand holding the handrail to ensure its cleanliness. On other occasions we flew into Tokyo, and whatever else was on the agenda, no visit was complete without a ride on the bullet train. One memorable trip was to the city of Kyoto where a walk through the Imperial Palace gardens was both moving and restorative to the weariness of the previous long flight. However, my body clock was telling me it was time for a change. And that is exactly what happened …

Having spotted a management notice in the corridors of Crew Reporting that they were looking for Concorde crew, I wasted no time in arranging a meeting with my cabin crew manager to see if I passed the grades to join the 'Elite Fleet'. Although I would miss the glamorous locations that the 747 flew to, I was not going to miss the brain-numbing time changes.

After an interview in which the annual reports on my standard of work had been scrutinised and a file of complimentary letters read through, I was accepted. There followed a week's Concorde familiarisation in the training centre near Heathrow Airport and our class of thirteen 'graduated' and were ready to fly the 'pocket rocket'. The instruction for this new work environment had included learning the fine wines and food served during the flight and, more importantly, the strict routines of

The last day of Concorde training group in 1981, receiving our Concorde wings.

cabin service. Even though I was used to working in first class on the 747 there were still big changes ahead – mainly the passenger number being up to 100 instead of twenty-four. There were also the safety procedures to learn and exams to pass.

As with every aircraft, one could not take to the skies without precise knowledge of the stowage of safety equipment and the evacuation drills. Concorde equipment was, as you would imagine, the very latest in technology. One of the situations that we had to be trained for was the evacuation of the aircraft on water. The theory was that if the aircraft had to land on water, the passengers would be directed out of the aircraft doors with their lifejackets already on but not inflated. (Lifejackets would be inflated once on the wing.) The plus side to all this was that the wings were so large that a full complement of 100 passengers could assemble on them and wait their turn to get into the life rafts that the crew would have dutifully inflated.

So in theory, we as crew would be faced with traumatised passengers tottering out onto the wings all dressed in the BA fashion statement of yellow lifejackets, distraught at having to leave behind their Manolo Blahnik shoes, laptops and Gucci handbags on an aircraft that they were now abandoning for a wet rubber inflatable and a ration of Mars Bars. It didn't bear thinking about!

The downside to this very hypothetical dire situation was that if Concorde had ever to land in rough seas in an emergency, it would have more than likely gone straight down to the bottom of the ocean. When I asked the flight crew about Concorde's abilities to land on water they were very cautious about the idea. They did admit that although the beautiful bird was built for speed at high altitude, its aquatic abilities were extremely limited and they would not have wanted to put them to the test. Whether Concorde could have remained afloat for very long, we shall thankfully never know.

When Concorde moved to short-haul operations in 1981, for reasons I will explain later, we also had to train to fly on the BAC 1-11, an aircraft that has now retired to sit in the Museum of the History of Flight (there is also one at Brooklands Museum in Surrey). I will always remember the day aboard a mock-up of this plane in the Safety Training Centre, when we were being given instruction on how to deploy the slides. I'm not sure what my face was registering – incredulity that such a bizarre method would pass aviation regulations or the giggle that I was suppressing at the thought of having to evacuate, slowly, a full load of passengers. The words in my head, to quote John McEnroe, were, 'You cannot be serious'.

I hope I will be forgiven by any devotees of the 1-11 who will probably be very upset that I could besmirch this aircraft. They will probably quote to me on the number of times its safety record passed with flying colours and that the procedures worked perfectly. The drill, however, was quite archaic after the Concorde and 747s. Speedy it was not. There were stairs for evacuation at the rear of the aircraft, but if the engines were on fire then you would have to exit at the front of the aircraft, which is where the slides were located in a hatch above the two exit doors. First, these had to be opened and lowered. Second, two very tall, very strong crew members (I was not in this category) had to lower a heavy canvas package onto the floor and uncover the slide. Third, two able-bodied volunteers (passengers, *not* crew – would they be entitled to a refund?) had to then scale down the side of the aircraft (rope provided) and hold out the slide for the passengers to flee the fire or whatever hazard had forced us to abandon the plane. This means of escape was never going to happen quickly and there was something quite genteel about the whole set-up. One can imagine the crew saying, 'One at a time please, and, sir/madam, we will be serving you tea on the tarmac shortly.'

THE SUPERSONIC EXPERIENCE – 'FLYING HOTEL' TO 'POCKET ROCKET'

Concorde was an entirely new working environment. The familiar spacious cabins of the 747s were replaced with a narrow, low-ceilinged interior (the cabin height being 6ft 5in (1.96m)) and grey leather seats that exuded exclusivity. This was more private jet than flying machine for the masses. With it came a new reverence for the job. Despite my seven years' flying experience I still remember being extremely nervous on my first Concorde flight.

Up until 1981 the Concorde crews led a pretty easy life. They worked, on average, a 7-hour week. The pay was comparatively low due to fewer overseas allowances, but the glamour stakes were high. When Concorde first started its commercial routes in 1976, the crew were regarded as pioneers. Julia van den Bosch, one of the original stewardesses who stayed on it until its retirement in 2003, recalls a publicity reception at the Dorchester Hotel in London. One of the guests, the Duchess of Argyll, came up to Julia and shook her by the hand. 'So brave,' she commented. 'You are so brave to fly on an aircraft to the edge of space.'

The British Airways long-haul flight rules (which included any flights outside of Europe) made provision that the cabin crews were entitled to four days off after a flight back to their London base. In the early days, Concorde came under this umbrella. This, of course, provided an envious lifestyle and one Cockney steward on short haul was known to refer to the Concorde crew as 'those from 'arrods whilst the rest of us were from Woolies'.

In the seventies and early eighties, the schedules to Washington included a five-day stopover. There were idyllic days in the summer of long lunches, picnics and rowing on the Potomac River. To while away the time the crews also got into a routine of making up afternoon tea for the incoming crew.

In New York there was a similar relaxed lifestyle. A leisurely crew breakfast in one of the local coffee shops was followed by shopping at Bloomingdales, Macy's and Korvettes, a visit to the Guggenheim and other galleries, long drawn out lunches at Tavern on the Green in Central Park and the lure of theatre, shows and opera in the evening. The Rainbow Room, Studio 54 and other famous hotspots were also on the crew agenda. In winter, the stewardesses' luggage contained exotic fur coats for the luncheon parties that followed their arrival into New York. On the fourth day they would fly home in 3 hours and 30 minutes, or less, to spend another four days unpacking their shopping and enjoying a pretty civilised home life.

The first stopover of a Concorde route to south-east Asia was the inaugural flight between London Heathrow (LHR) and Bahrain (BAH) on 21 January 1976. The route was mainly overland, forcing the Concorde to fly at subsonic speeds on large portions of the London–Bahrain sector. But the aircraft still managed to save around 2 hours and 30 minutes over the regular flights with a Mach 0.95 cruise speed. In December 1977, three flights a week to Singapore commenced but were stopped after just three return flights following complaints from the Malaysian Government regarding the noise over the Straits of Malacca.

The Bahrain to Singapore trip for flight and cabin crew was nine days and run jointly with Singapore Airlines. The flight crew and operational crew were British Airways whilst the cabin crew was 50 per cent Singaporean girls who, incidentally, never failed to win over the flight crew and no doubt added extra exotica to their flying schedule. The aircraft used for this route (G-BOAD) was painted with the Singapore Airlines livery on one side and British Airways on the other.

In 1979 these services were resumed, this time avoiding Malaysia, but sadly the plug was pulled on this service in November 1980 as the revenue figures showed the route had low passenger numbers and was losing £2 million a year. It was rumoured that after the showing of the controversial film *Death of a Princess* on British TV, the Saudi Government declined to have Concorde and this service was also halted.

The flights to Dallas/Fort Worth in 1979 became a loss-making route and were cancelled in 1980. Concorde was now left with destinations to New York, Washington, Miami and various charters. Air France discontinued their service to Washington in 1982; from then on New York became its only scheduled destination.

By 1981 the future of Concorde looked bleak. The government had lost money on Concorde operations annually and it was mooted that it would cease to fly. The government gave the airline two years to turn the loss around. The chairman of British Airways, Sir John King, remained convinced that Concorde was a premier product and underpriced. Market research revealed that many high-flying businessmen did not actually buy their own tickets, this task was delegated to their PA or secretary. Therefore, many did not know the cost and, when asked, thought the fare was much higher than it actually was. Ticket prices were then raised to match these perceptions. Sir John persuaded the government to sell Concorde outright to his airline for a mere £16.5 million plus the first year's profits. In two years Concorde changed its fortunes – it started making big profits.

Timing, as they say, is everything in life and it soon became apparent that the exclusive Concorde crew lifestyle was neither viable for the company nor realistically feasible to run conjointly with the other hard-working fleets of BA. When I joined the Concorde fleet in 1981 it had been operating for five years and a cost-saving exercise was about to be implemented. British Airways crew management, in their wisdom, decided to change the flying regulations and bring Concorde working hours in line with the rest of the BA fleets (an 'arrod's–Woolies merger, perhaps?).

I had six weeks of the 'old style life' before the merger. From then on Concorde was switched to the short-haul fleet under the auspices of shorter flying hours compared with those of the long-haul flights. With the 3-hour 30-minute flying time across the Atlantic, the cabin crews were now able to work the next day, forgoing their four days off previously guaranteed under long-haul rules. They could now fly six consecutive days, and this could include another Concorde flight across the Atlantic, or a BAC 1-11 or 737 flights into Europe. This now became a matter of flying hours and not distance and the six-day short-haul roster came into force, allowing three days off in the UK after this work period. And we were effectively trained to fly on three aircraft.

In the early days of the changeover, I was one of the few left who had flown on the aircraft whilst under the long-haul agreement. Many of the original Concorde stewardesses, having rightly guessed that this was the end of a very comfortable era, had left under the new rules. Their elitist lifestyle had become part of Concorde history, and so a new intake of short-haul crew was trained for the Concorde operation. The more experienced of us were called upon by the office hierarchy to initiate the new recruits and I found myself flying across the Atlantic on six consecutive days. Six crossings in six days was a tall order and I was completely exhausted at the end of my 18,000-mile commuting week. Fortunately this situation did not last for long.

Julia van den Bosch, Concorde's longest serving stewardess, sitting in the engine housing. (Courtesy of Julia van den Bosch)

Louise Brown sitting with a colleague in the engine housing. (Courtesy of Louise Brown)

The stress and workload for the new crews and experienced hands that ensued in those initial weeks were not ideal. The short-haul crew, in fairness, had not been trained to do a first-class service before their Concorde training so their learning curves were steeper than Concorde's climb rate after take-off with an empty load. They very quickly learnt that speed was of the essence and landing with meal trays still in their hands was not the best way to arrive at their destination.

Despite our reputation for superlative professionalism there was inevitably the odd calamity, and not only during the change over from long-haul crew to short-haul crew. We can all recall the landings when the reverse thrust of the engines brought the aircraft to a shuddering halt on the runway. During this procedure on a number of occasions one of the trolleys would jump out of its restraining straps and trundle off on its own journey down the aisle gaining momentum with the speed of the aircraft's braking. One trolley, on such an occasion, even managed to reach the flight deck door. Strapped in as we were, the crew could do little to halt is wayward path. I often wondered what the passengers made of this.

THE WORKING DAY:
BEHIND THE SCENES

A cabin crew day started with checking in at the British Airways Crew Reporting Office based on the perimeter road at Heathrow. In the seventies and eighties this was a utilitarian building that resembled a cross between an enlarged army Nissen hut and a small industrial unit. British Airways finally upped their image in the nineties by replacing it with a huge, super smart, state-of-the-art building with blue glass windows called the Compass Centre. The flight crews before this had their own check-in office at Terminal 1.

Living in Kew, my trip to the airport was a short drive on the M4. However, there were crew members who travelled far greater distances to operate their flights. Some commuted from Manchester, Jersey, Scotland and even France.

Getting to the airport was not without its tense moments. If you were just a few minutes late without informing the check-in staff (and there were no mobile phones then) you were automatically stood down from the flight and replaced by a standby crew member at Crew Reporting. This had its advantages on some of the long, unpopular long-haul night flights, but not on Concorde.

Having checked in at the reporting desk and collected the internal mail that included future flying schedules or rosters, the crew assembled in one of the allocated briefing rooms for a 20-minute briefing by the cabin service director (or CSD as we called him). He would cast a beady eye around to make sure everyone was properly attired and smartly dressed. The Concorde uniforms were the same as the other fleets but the hats, which sometimes rested in the hat rack for embarkation of passengers on other flights, were obligatory on Concorde, as were the white gloves. Personal appearance was absolutely of key importance and special care was taken with this. No scrappy hairdos or overdue haircuts were permitted.

In general, the more 'easy-going' the cabin service director was the more we relaxed and committed to enjoying our flight. Those who 'nit-picked' and took the job too seriously were often an adverse influence on the crew. If we were relaxed it would reflect on our initial meeting with the passengers. And, being the consummate professionals that we were, the relaxed attitude in no way reflected on our prompt, efficient service.

We would be assigned or allowed to choose our working positions in the cabin. These would be either in the front or rear cabin or the galleys, one at the front and one at the rear. Although the CSD was ultimately responsible for the whole of the aircraft and its passengers, he worked in the front cabin and the purser was in charge of the rear backed up by a team of two other crew in each cabin.

During the briefing the CSD would give us the flight time, the name of the captain, first officer and engineer and the type of meal to be served. There were invariably special requests for different dietary foods and these were pointed out.

Working in the galley meant responsibility for the timings and cooking of the meals but did not require the smiling, friendly persona presented to the passengers for the whole flight. We all had an off day now and again where we would prefer to do galley duties, unless of course the movie or rock star of our dreams was on board!

I have been asked on many occasions if there were two classes on the aircraft. The front cabin seated forty passengers and the rear sixty, but both were exactly the same in standard and type of service. There was, however, a snob value to sitting in seat 1A or 1D at the very front, which the regular clientele competed for. The royals always sat there as it was a quieter seat and provided the most privacy.

During the crew briefing famous names, politicians, top executives and regular clientele who were travelling with us were also brought to our attention. It always added an extra buzz to the working day if there was a well-known face on board. If it was a movie or rock star we were always curious to meet them in the flesh. Names such as Barry Gibb, Robert de Niro, Tom Cruise or Paul McCartney invariably brought a smile to the female faces at the briefing. One had to compare this to my previous occupation of teaching – where would one meet such luminaries in the everyday workplace? Could one go home and say 'Well guess who came into my "office" this morning?' Henry Kissinger, Michael Jackson or Elizabeth Taylor?

After the briefing, a crew bus would transport us across to Terminal 3 where Concorde was being prepared for its flight. A bevy of busy ground engineers, catering, cargo and fuel trucks were all part of the activity that surrounded the 'tethered bird' waiting patiently for its release into supersonic flight.

Once aboard we introduced ourselves to the three flight crew, who by this time were well into their preflight checks. In the galleys, hot drinks were prepared for them and the menus were unwrapped, along with newspapers and magazines which were prepared for presentation to the passengers. The drinks trolleys and meals were checked, and plastic covers lifted off the meal trays and canapés. The toilets and cabins were carefully scrutinised for tidiness and cleanliness. The CSD would perform a thorough check of safety equipment before the passengers' coats arrived.

THE FLYING WARDROBE

In the seventies and eighties when consummate wealth reached its highest amongst the Concorde jet set, their opulent fur coats and designer outdoor wear would be wheeled onto the aircraft on a hanging rail. These would be carefully stowed into a compact wardrobe area. I emphasise 'carefully' because some of the animal pelts were worth a year's salary to some of us lesser mortals. Whether flying to or leaving New York or Washington, where the temperatures in winter could drop to well below zero, the minks were a pretty common item. There was more often than not a quick appraisal of those we thought the most chic. Sometimes we went a step further and modelled them, much to the amusement of the male crew.

The men's coats and jackets were equally appealing and made of the softest wool or cashmere. Designer names such as Burberry, Ralph Lauren and Yves St Laurent were all familiar labels. For a first-time crew on Concorde this was a taste of who and what was to come, and the passengers invariably oozed wealth. This was no ordinary air travel. The clientele dressed for the flight in exclusive designer clothes and jewels that would collectively warrant a Securicor van at their destination. Designer handbags and briefcases were of the finest leather or crocodile. Not only were our guests well dressed but the cabin air would be scented with the most exclusive aftershaves and perfumes. If money had a smell, this was it.

An interesting change was noted by one of my colleagues, who commented that after the champagne-drinking, mink-wearing hedonism of the eighties there followed a period of more austere outdoor wear. The ostentatious minks were replaced by regular coats and instead of the champagne quaffing high-flyers, a more demure breed of Perrier drinkers took their place.

However, during my time in the eighties, there was one flight when a female passenger came aboard wearing a three-quarter length mink coat. This was unusual, as most were glad to part company with their coats before boarding the aircraft. When I asked her if she would like me to hang up her coat she politely refused and, to the crews' incredulity, sat through the whole flight wearing it. We could only assume that it was so expensive she didn't want to lose sight of it.

When we landed in London, it was not unusual for customs to bring sniffer dogs onto the aircraft to check for drugs. On this occasion the dog grew very excited at the seat at the rear of the aircraft where this particular female passenger had been sitting. The customs were pretty convinced this was a 'drug seat'. We never did find out whether HM Customs & Excise caught up with the passenger in the customs hall to check the exact contents of her coat.

Another incident regarding fur coats happened whilst I was working on the 747 fleet and before I transferred to Concorde. We were travelling from New York to London and again a lady decided to wear her thick fur coat all the way to London. As I was passing her seat during the meal service I happened to notice her 'feeding' her coat a morsel of steak!

Unsure how to ask her why she was feeding her coat and taken aback at what I had just seen, I relayed what I had seen to the purser in charge of the cabin. Before congratulating myself on my astute powers of observation, I accompanied the purser to the seat. He grew suspicious when he detected a movement from within the coat. 'Are you concealing something in your coat?' he politely asked. The sweet old lady timidly admitted her cover was blown and showed us a miniature dog curled up inside a large inside pocket. This, of course, was strictly illegal.

The captain almost blew a gasket upon being told he had pro-
hibited items in the cabin and instructed the dog be removed
immediately and isolated from its owner. One can only assume
that this incident would involve a lot of paperwork for a tired
flight crew arriving into London, hence his irascibility.

Five minutes later this poor pooch was transferred to an
upturned wire drinks basket and sat bewildered and shivering
in its new 'home' by a drafty aircraft door. As a fervent animal
lover I was extremely upset by his poor treatment. Not only
had the dog been removed from the warmth and comfort of
its owner's fur coat, but it was confused by its noisy environment so, seeking to give it some solace, I put my hand through
the cage to stroke it. My kind gesture was rebuffed with a nasty
bite to the finger!

Little did I know that informing the purser of the dog's
response would land me in a lot of trouble. Having relayed
the incident to the captain, the purser told me to report to the
flight deck immediately. I was summarily interrogated by a
very cross captain. 'What were you doing going near that dog?'
He fumed. 'Why did you touch it?' Innocently I defended my
case by saying the animal looked lonely and frightened. Then,
seeing this was going to land me in trouble, I mentioned that
it was only a little nip. 'Lucky for you then,' he replied tetchily,
'because if it had drawn blood, you, along with the dog, would
both be turned over to the quarantine authorities.' How unfair,
I thought, as I returned to my work, that a little kindness had
landed me in such trouble.

FLIGHT 001 IS NOW
READY FOR BOARDING

Concorde had its own check-in desk at Heathrow and this was where the exclusive experience for the supersonic passenger began. It was quick, it was smart and it was the queue (if indeed there ever was one) that every airline passenger wanted to join. No queuing at McDonald's or Costa Coffee for these fortunates. The Concorde boarding pass opened up the glitz of exclusive airline comfort. The luxury of the departure lounge offered newspapers, telephones, fax machines (before laptop and mobile phone days), television and secretarial services. An abundance of drinks, champagne, canapés, snacks, fruit and coffee were also available.

Twenty minutes before the flight's departure, the passengers would be escorted onto Concorde. The crew's first job was to give them a warm welcome and if we had flown with them before we always greeted them personally by name. Concorde had, as David Frost said, 'an exclusive private club atmosphere'. It was small, it was friendly and whenever you could you addressed the passenger by their name.

Storage space was minimal so it was often quite a feat to stow the carry-on luggage in the hat racks. One of the most memorable items I have offered to assist with was the Stradivarius violin belonging to Sir Yehudi Menuhin. Sir Yehudi informed me very politely that he could stow this without any help. He and his wife were the most charming, unpretentious couple, and I still have his signed menu.

On another flight, Sir Yehudi accepted the offer for the violin to be stowed in the rear wardrobe. Julia van den Bosch, who was the purser at the time, recalls how she took the priceless instrument wrapped in a cloth cover and stowed it very carefully in the rear wardrobe. This was checked several times during the flight and it appeared that no harm could possibly come to it. Towards the end of the flight, however, a passenger sitting in the rear seat in front of the wardrobe was in a hurry to go to the bathroom and, forgetting the tray that was on his lap, leapt up and the glass of wine that was on it became airborne … and flew into the wardrobe. Julia was horrified to discover the cloth covering one of the most expensive string instruments in the world had not escaped the deluge of flying wine.

Summoning up all her reserves, she broke the news to the 'maestro'. Sir Yehudi wasted no time in getting out of his seat and hotfooting it down the aisle to inspect the damage. To his and everyone else's huge relief the violin inside the case was untouched. Perhaps that is why, on the flight on which I met him, he decided the best place for his instrument was in the overhead locker right above his head and away from any possible calamities.

On a flight to Washington I was once handed three bottles of wine by two Arab passengers and expressly asked to take great care of them. These bottles weren't ordinary duty-free. The Arabs informed me of their cost – £1,000 apiece, which in today's money equivalent would probably be nearer £3,000. They were duly stowed away with immense care.

On one occasion, after the passengers had boarded the aircraft, an aircraft dispatcher (or 'red cap', as we called them) came on with a package under his arm wrapped in brown paper. He casually he told me this was the cargo the captain was expecting on the flight deck. This being an unusual procedure, I asked the red cap what was in the brown paper.

'A Cezanne,' he said with a wink.

Sure enough, when I went onto the flight deck the captain asked me to remove the brown paper and there it was. The first and last time I ever held a genuine Cezanne.

Julia van den Bosch recalls an Arab charter where a live falcon came on board and was taken up to the flight deck for the duration of the flight. She reminisced, thinking that if the aircraft had gone down, one of the last things that may have been recorded in the black box would have been the panicky squawk of a bird!

Once settled in their seats, the passengers would be offered vintage champagne and soft drinks, hot towels, menus and newspapers. An order would be taken for drinks and cocktails to be served straight after take-off. Even for these wealthy and widely travelled people, the beginning of the supersonic experience was a moment of excitement. Despite their feigned nonchalance as they tried to read their newspapers, few passengers could disguise their pleasure and anticipation as the seat belts were buckled up, followed by the safety demonstration and the preflight welcome, giving the flying speed of 1,650mph and a flying time to New York of 3 hours and the last numerical was given in exact minutes (normal range between 20 and 24 minutes). This preflight routine could never compare to flying in other aircraft. The suspense was palpable as Concorde pushed back from its stand and taxied down passed the stands of its bigger brothers.

The first flight (or supernumerary) for any cabin crew on Concorde was always special. There was the excitement of flying supersonic for the first time, plus the prestige of working amongst a very exclusive clientele. The experience of my first flight more than exceeded my expectations. Suddenly one was entering a new working environment. With it came a new reverence for the job. It was 'back to school' again, and the crew I flew with on my first flight took on the role of school prefects who I revered and adhered to their every word. First-time flight nerves also kicked in.

The captains were very kind to the new recruits and invariably offered them a seat on the flight deck for take-off and landing, which again was a pretty special way to start one's new working environment. At the end of the flight, the new crew were given a certificate with all the crew names signed on it.

My supernumerary had a special significance as I was eased in very gently to the whole routine. There were only a few passengers on board, but sitting at the rear of the aircraft was Mick Jagger, along with ten other passengers at most. The purser mentioned to him that it was my first flight and Mick kindly volunteered to have his photo taken with me and signed a menu. I met him several times on flights after that, and he was often accompanied by Gerry Hall.

LIFE AT THE SHARP END

> It is a little known fact that there are more US astronauts on the planet than there are Concorde pilots …

I would often ask to go up on the flight deck for take-off and landing and the flight crew never seemed to mind. The supernumerary seat was next to the engineer and directly behind the captain. It was folded up in a convoluted manner that required a knack to unfold it, which I never seemed to master. However, once seated the engineer would ensure that I was properly strapped in. We shared many giggles as one of the lap straps had to go from the base of the seat between my legs and up to the locking system at chest height. This was fine if one was wearing trousers, as we could with one of our uniform designs, but with a skirt, dignity was cast aside.

The engineers invariably enjoyed the struggle of fixing it into position. The undignified crotch strap was attached to a five-point harness with two shoulder straps and a waist strap. This was quite a procedure and I did wonder how the female royals who visited the flight deck coped with this. I later found out that Princess Margaret was given a tea towel to place over the hitched up area of her dress, thereby preserving her modesty.

Whilst I enjoyed the view from the cockpit window, the flight engineer would undertake another thirty checks, including the transfer of fuel from a rear trim tank for use before take-off. The captain would be steering the aircraft by means of a small handle on the side panel. No mean feat, as the nose wheel was 38ft behind him and the main wheels were 97ft behind. Unlike any other aircraft, Concorde had a springy feel to it in the cockpit during taxiing as the long narrow fuselage flexed over any bump on the taxi, or runway.

So, for 10 minutes of my working day I would sometimes swap the back end of the 'office' for the front end, and this was without doubt the most exhilarating one. For those watching take-off from the ground it was a unique experience, especially at night. The red glow of the afterburners shedding 30ft of flames from the four engines was an unforgettable sight and a reminder of Concorde's similarity to the space shuttle blast from Cape Canaveral.

Of the many take-offs I experienced from the flight deck, leaving Miami one beautiful morning was a sublime experience. In the cramped space surrounded by dials and three busy flight crew at work, one could fully appreciate the technology of Concorde. As we edged back from the stand many cameras and binoculars were aimed at the sleek fuselage and as we taxied to the runway a Pan Am captain was heard to request a delay in take-off so he could watch us depart.

Pre-take-off checks complete, speed and heading confirmed to the control tower, engines to be throttled back 48 seconds after take-off. All was ready for our departure to Washington. The first officer even had time to comment on a battered old aircraft poking out of a hangar. 'That would make a good investment for you, Sally,' he remarked.

Lining up on the runway with only twenty-four passengers aboard, we reached 225mph in 18 seconds and lifted off gracefully, climbing high and fast into a dazzling aquamarine sky. Below us, the freeway was busy with morning traffic, the waterways had a steady flow of cruisers heading towards the ocean. Empty beaches appeared before us and then the ocean, glinting like a sea of diamonds. We must have looked a beautiful sight as we climbed away from the city.

The Washington to Miami service was stopped in 1991 due to low passenger numbers and, from a crew point of view, it

Mach 2.

was missed. Miami gave us that glimpse of winter sunshine on our few hours off. The Washington service finished in 1994, also due to poor passenger loads.

INTO THE STRATOSPHERE, THE CURVATURE OF THE EARTH AND TO NEW YORK

During the taxi to its departure point on the runway Concorde would burn almost 1.2 tons of fuel, or 2 per cent of its total capacity. I remember on one occasion, when flying out of New York, Concorde was sitting on the tarmac for 20 minutes. The fuel tanks by this time were registering a drop significant enough for us to return to the stand so that we could be topped up to ensure a safe passage home. Concorde had to have fuel reserves of 45 minutes – either for a holding pattern or a diversion to another airport. In spite of the amount of fuel the aircraft burnt even whilst on the runway, air traffic control did not give Concorde priority for take-off. The New York authorities, however, did allow Concorde to queue jump when it came to landing at John F. Kennedy Airport.

One Concorde captain, who was not so cautious about the fuel reserves after leaving New York, ignored the advice of the flight engineer to divert to Shannon to refuel and pressed on to London. Punctuality was more of an issue than 'gas in the tanks' on this occasion. The Concorde did land safely at Heathrow but ran out of fuel after leaving the runway. That was a close shave for the company. Perhaps lawsuits would have been issued faster than a Concorde take-off had the truth come to light.

Listening to the conversations between the captain and control tower through a pair of headphones was also part of the take-off perk and it was fascinating to listen in to other aircraft and the directives of the air traffic controller. The captain would wait for our call sign and permission to take off. The calm resonant voice of the air traffic controller directing the take-off procedure would come through the headset: 'Okay Speedbird 193 cleared for take-off.'

You could almost envisage the other aircraft waiting for their turn, bowing in deference to their faster cousin. It is also pretty hard to put into words that moment when take-off clearance was granted. The captain would engage the throttles and as they went fully forward, there would be a slight nudge in the back as acceleration gathered pace down the runway. Again another surge of excitement and thrill that in 30 seconds one would become airborne and soar into the skies. No lumbering down the runway 747-style for what seemed like forever, to Staines and beyond. Concorde was like a caged bird. As soon as she saw the runway she couldn't wait for her release to be airborne.

The take-off speed was 225mph (223km/h) faster than any other commercial aircraft. Concorde burnt 25,629 litres of fuel per hour.

Leaving London's Heathrow Airport the captain would, by law, have to throttle back for noise abatement. Even with the afterburners switched off, the climb would be 1,000ft per minute. Gaining height steadily, the nose and visor were raised. Life in the cockpit became quieter. Climbing over Reading at 8,000ft the full power of the four Rolls-Royce Olympus engines would be initiated again and the climb speed at that point would be 3,000ft per minute. At 28,000ft the passengers were glued to the Mach meters at the front of each cabin. At this height we would be cruising at Mach 0.95, just below the speed of sound, and flying over the Bristol Channel.

Once clear of the Welsh coastline, the reheat switches would be flicked on by the engineer, two at a time. The afterburners would kick in and the Mach meters in the cabin would clock up Mach 1. The pre-lunch cocktails would have been served and for first-time supersonic flyers they would invariably toast the 'Mach 1 Experience' with a glass of champagne. A mere 34 minutes after take-off, Concorde had reached Mach 2. We were now streaking across the Atlantic at 1,350mph – a mile every 2.7 seconds – and at 58,000ft in our 'pocket rocket'.

During the winter evening service to New York, we would take off in the dark and, heading west, we would experience a spectacular golden glow 'sunrise'. The aircraft flying faster than the rotation of the earth would catch up the sun and we could watch it 'rising' and then setting again before we landed. This was a completely unique experience. Before the supersonic experience no man had seen the sun 'rise' in the west.

Turbulence, fortunately, was rare at this height. We were above the jet stream and thunderstorms. There was no sense of movement. If there was a time and place where man felt small this would be it. The curvature of the earth in its midnight blue mantle could be seen quite clearly and if one had time to pause and reflect it would be to wonder at the beauty and magnificence of it all. We were on the edge of space, leaving behind the busy life of one continent to arrive at another. In the meantime, there was 3,400 miles of ocean below, the sky around us and a small aircraft catching up the rotation of the earth.

Did we ever see anything below us at that altitude? We passed over the occasional transatlantic jet which appeared to be going backwards in comparison to our speed (800mph faster) and our height (20,000ft higher). The Atlantic Ocean always appeared a smooth shade of blue-grey. No waves were visible from this height, but I do remember a brief glimpse of the *Queen Elizabeth 2* (*QE2*). The flight crew had been in radio communication with her and as we passed over her at Mach 2 we were able to see her very briefly, a tiny sliver of the hull 11 miles below us. I believe on this occasion the captains discussed what was on their lunch menus – the *QE2*'s side of the conversation being somewhat lengthier than that of the captain on our flight.

A WELL-STOCKED WINE CELLAR AND FOOD FIT FOR A PRINCE

On the 747 first-class service to New York, a five-course meal was served to a maximum of twenty-four passengers at a leisurely pace. Time was not an issue as we had 7 hours and 30 minutes to feed and look after our passengers.

Now, multiply the seating in Concorde's flying restaurant by four, divide the time by two, cut the working space by four, and the maths work out as pretty much impossible on paper. There must have been a lot of head-scratching in the logistics department when the meal plans in this five-star 'space rocket' were devised.

Service would begin immediately after the seatbelt sign was switched off, the drinks order having been taken on a notepad prior to take-off. The cocktails, expertly prepared by the galley steward, would be served to passengers on a silver tray. These were accompanied by prettily decorated bite-size canapés of caviar, goose galantine, prawns and smoked salmon.

Our repertoire of cocktails sounds somewhat dated now compared to the kaleidoscopic lethal concoctions found in bars today. Our cocktail choice of a Manhattan, Old-Fashioned and Highball, Americano and Negroni belonged to the seventies 'James Bond' era and the genteel habitués of the Waldorf Astoria and the Rainbow Room. Uncomplicated cocktails they were, but no less effective. They were not for the faint-hearted, especially at high altitude. A champagne cocktail, a mix of champagne, brandy, sugar and Angostura bitters, could have warranted a 'proceed with caution' notice. More popular were the standard no-frills Bloody Mary or dry Martini.

For the older English generation on charters, who made Concorde their once-in-a-lifetime experience, the tipple for the demure old ladies was often a port and lemonade, sherry or sweet Martini, no doubt a reflection back to the high day and holiday mood when those drinks were a 'push the boat out' sort of moment. For the men, they were happy with cans of beer after the celebratory glass of champagne.

The wine and drinks menu was, however, a huge temptation for the wine connoisseur, regular commuter or first-timer to the Concorde experience. It was a supremely difficult task to resist such expensive vintage wines, champagnes and top label spirits. However, most of the regulars were well aware of the dangers of mixing flying at high altitude and the high alcohol content of cocktails. They preferred to sip at the expensive wines and champagne. Invariably a neatly manicured finger would be pointed to the glass for the exact amount to top up and one dare not exceed the limit of the finger pointing!

During this part of the service, Concorde held the reputation for being the fastest, highest and most expensive cocktail bar in the world. The view out of the windows was pretty spectacular too. The earth's curvature could be quite clearly seen and at 11 miles high the sky is a deep indigo.

After a second drinks round, the glasses would be cleared away. The meal set-up was preceded by laying a Damask tablecloth on the fold-up tables in front of the passengers followed by a tray with cutlery, a miniature Royal Doulton condiment set and linen napkins. The cold starter course was usually seafood – crab legs, lobster or salmon. One such starter was described as 'Fresh Maine lobster and barquette of Sevruga caviar garnished with artichoke, lemon and mayonnaise', and always popular. Iranian caviar also came on the menu at regular intervals and was served in small sealed pots along with a garnish of onion and chopped egg white and yolk as an accompaniment. (Nothing could beat the sheer hedonism of getting home after a flight and spooning up the contents of one of those jars, that is, if one was lucky enough to find one unopened after the meal service.)

This would be followed by a main course presented on Royal Doulton china and delivered to the passenger on a silver tray. There was no handling of plates by hand. The plate was transferred from tray to table using a 'spong' (a name and method peculiar to airlines, I believe). A spong is a neat, long-handled serving tool with a lip at the end that holds the dish in place whilst it is carefully being transferred to the passenger tray. In my experience it was foolproof and I never heard of any crew member dropping a plate using this sturdy, reliable piece of equipment.

The main courses were a gourmet's delight. The menu out of London might include an 'English Game Pie prepared from marinated venison, pheasant and morel mushrooms'. Turbot was often a favourite on the menu. The American pronunciation was often to leave off the last syllable. Turbot would invariably be pronounced 'turbo' and a fillet steak would be 'fillee' (cue smile from the stewardess). I did have one American passenger who pronounced pheasant with a hard 'p' (as in the poor, working on the land variety). I was tempted ask her how she would like her country bumpkin served up. But at times like these diplomacy prevails. I don't think America have 'pheasants' (the people variety) in their countryside. I cannot remember an instance of the American species. Did they have the dubious promotion of 'farm workers'? If not, I stand corrected.

The menu choice of steak would include dishes such as Tournedos Périgord, 'a fillet of prime beef grilled and coated with a rich dark sauce prepared with truffles from Périgord accompanied by buttered leaf spinach, artichokes, tomato and wild rice pilaf'. A spring menu might include lamb, under the grand title of 'Noisettes d'agneau Prince Orloff: small steaklets of lamb seared on a hot griddle [naturally not on the aircraft] topped with a mixture of shredded ox tongue, pimentos, onions and cream served with Madeira sauce'.

Game was frequently included in the menu. Noisettes of venison with chestnuts came in a rich game sauce and was garnished with Morello cherries. Pheasant, grouse, duck and roast quail also made appearances on the winter menu. Although quail stuffed with foie gras had a novelty value, this was not a particular favourite with the passengers as it was small and boney. However the jus, a wine sauce again prepared with truffles from Périgord, was delicious.

On one occasion when this was included on the menu we had a steward on the crew who was of half Greek origin. The Greeks are well known for their consumption of anything small, airborne and with two wings. After the meal service was finished our steward who, I would add, had a great sense of humour, explained to us that in Greece the bird was eaten whole without removing any of the bones. The comment was greeted by a cynical 'Oh yes' from the three stewardesses in the galley.

'Okay I'll show you,' he replied. Removing one of the remaining birds from the oven he chomped his way casually through it and swallowed it, bones and all. Our eyes were popping and we were left in awe and admiration for his sturdy Greek digestive system!

On the 10.30 a.m. flight from London, and on the morning departure from New York, a brunch was served. This could include kippers coated in breadcrumbs and a pan-fried, fluffy omelette, or the 'Concorde Brunch' of pork loin, pork sausages accompanied by button mushrooms and Anna potatoes. And by the time the passengers arrived in New York at 9.30 a.m. local time, they were in time for another late breakfast.

There was always a variety of seasonal salads to accompany the main course, aptly called on some flights 'a millionaire's salad' and served with a choice of dressing. A selection of French and English cheeses followed the main course in true French tradition. These could include cheeses such as Tomme de Savoie, English Stilton or Cheddar served with vintage port. The meal finished with a delicate and refreshing dessert. This usually included a fresh fruit ingredient such as fresh pineapple and figs served in a brandy and passion fruit syrup set on a base of macaroon, or a seasonal fruit salad served with kirsch.

Having cleared the remains of the meal service, the crew would commence a tea and coffee service accompanied by friandises – rich chocolate petits fours and mints – as the finale to this fine-dining experience.

The team of chefs who would prepare the menus, which changed weekly, would be highly distinguished. Michel and Albert Roux, whose restaurants included Le Gavroche in London and the Waterside Inn at Bray, were two of the chefs who designed menus for British Airways First Class and Concorde. Anton Mossimann, Shaun Hill, Richard Corrigan, Burton Race and Mark Edwards, Liam Tomlin and Claudia Fleming also had input over the years.

A selection of menus.

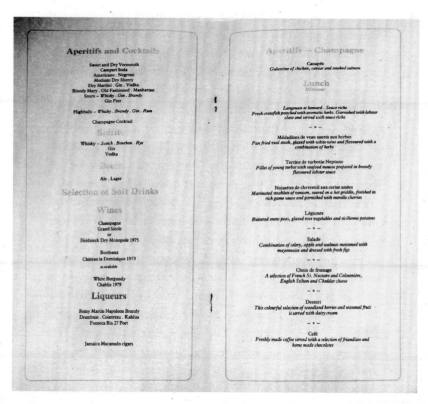

Aperitifs and Cocktails

Sweet and Dry Vermouth
Campari Soda
Americano . Negroni
Medium Dry Sherry
Dry Martini . Gin . Vodka
Bloody Mary . Old Fashioned . Manhattan
Sours – *Whisky . Gin . Brandy*
Gin Fizz

Highballs – *Whisky . Brandy . Gin . Rum*

Champagne Cocktail

Spirits

Whisky – *Scotch . Bourbon . Rye*
Gin
Vodka

Beers

Ale . Lager

Selection of Soft Drinks

Wines

Champagne
Grand Siècle
or
Heidsieck Dry Monopole 1975

Bordeaux
Château la Dominique 1973
as available

White Burgundy
Chablis 1979

Liqueurs

Remy Martin Napoleon Brandy
Drambuie . Cointreau . Kahlua
Fonseca Bin 27 Port

Jamaica Macanudo cigars

Aperitifs – Champagne

Canapés
Galantine of chicken, caviar and smoked salmon

Lunch
Déjeuner

Langouste et homard . Sauce riche
Fresh crawfish poached with aromatic herbs. Garnished with lobster claw and served with sauce riche

– * –

Médaillons de veau sautés aux herbes
Pan fried veal steak, glazed with white wine and flavoured with a combination of herbs

Terrine de turbotin Neptune
Fillet of young turbot with seafood mousse prepared in brandy flavoured lobster sauce

Noisettes de chevreuil aux cerise amère
Marinated steaklets of venison, seared on a hot griddle, finished in rich game sauce and garnished with morello cherries

Légumes
Buttered snow peas, glazed root vegetables and sicilienne potatoes

– * –

Salade
Combination of celery, apple and walnuts moistened with mayonnaise and dressed with fresh figs

– * –

Choix de fromage
A selection of French St. Nectaire and Coloumière, English Stilton and Cheddar cheese

– * –

Dessert
This colourful selection of woodland berries and seasonal fruit is served with dairy cream

– * –

Café
Freshly made coffee served with a selection of friandises and home made chocolates

Menu centre-spread.

On one occasion, Albert and Michel Roux were passengers on one of my flights to the USA. I felt extremely apprehensive as I served them one of their creations! Would it be the right temperature, would it be cooked to the perfection that they demanded in their kitchens? However, they were both very complimentary in their comments and smiled appreciatively. They were happy that we had done a good job.

The wines were of a standard that would make the most avid wine buff salivate in wine heaven. In the 1980s the champagne offered on the flights would be a vintage Cuvée de Rene Lalou Millésimé, described on the menu as a 'prince amongst champagnes – a privilege to drink and a rare gift to receive'. Another was Champagne Louis Heidsieck Dry Monopole 1975. One champagne of particular interest was Laurent-Perrier Grand Siècle in a uniquely shaped green bottle. This shape dated back to one used in the time of Louis XIV and the champagne was a blend of three vintages. In the early days of Concorde, Dom Perignon was served and, no doubt, in a class of its own.

The wines were pretty exceptional too and all of superior vintage. The red wine could be a Château Latour, one of the great wines of the Bordeaux region. The Les Forts de Latour 1981 is a Cabernet Sauvignon Merlot from the Pauillac region of France (the average price is now between £77 and £100 a bottle). Another excellent red wine was a Château Brane-Cantenac Margaux 1979, a wine from the Haut Medoc region of Bordeaux. A Château Cantemerle 1974, from the same region, also featured on the menu.

The white wines that would accompany such delights as a fricassee of fruits de mer or a lobster Newburg could be a 1982 Meursault or a Labouré-Roi Meursault 1985. Another favourite with passengers was a Puligny-Montrachet 1980 from the village famous for producing two of the world's greatest wines, Le Montrachet and Chevalier-Montrachet. A Chablis Premier Cru 'La Fourchaume' 1983, a classical Pinot

Chardonnay grape from one of the four best premier cru vineyards, was also served.

The wines, of which there would only be one of each type on board (i.e. one red, one white and one champagne), were presented to the passenger from a wine basket. It must have been a difficult choice for the executive commuters flying to New York to attend high-powered meetings to resist the wines on offer.

The saddest part about these expensive and classic vintage wines was the wastage. During the approach to our destination, any remaining wine had to be tipped down the sink. Even a bottle opened for half a glass of wine had to be disposed of. No, we didn't cry, but it almost brought tears to the eyes as the vintage champagne and wines disappeared down the sink.

There was a good selection of liqueurs and a Remy Martin Napoleon brandy offered with coffee. Before the 'no smoking' rule on aircraft came into effect, cigars were also offered with the coffee service. These would be Jamaican Macanudos and, whilst many of the male passengers enjoyed them, it wasn't so pleasant for the crew struggling through a fog of heavy aromatic cigar smoke. Thankfully, times have changed in the aircraft environment and the crews are no longer subjected to passive smoking hazards.

If the transatlantic flights were 100 per cent full, which they rarely were, the cabin crew were under a lot of pressure to get the service completed in time. Serving a gourmet dining experience to 100 passengers, where the service had to appear unhurried and calm, was achievable, but there were times when the last trays were being stowed as the landing lights of the runway came into view. The pulse was racing and the adrenalin pumping and often we would have wished to go and ask the captain to do another circuit to allow us to finish clearing away!

However, we took great delight in announcing the flight time to the last minute, and depending on the winds, this would vary on a regular basis between 3 hours 20 minutes and 3 hours 24 minutes. The captain was always very pleased to announce if we had beaten the projected flight time. Each crew member had a personal best for the Atlantic crossing and I remember mine from New York to London was 2 hours and 56 minutes.

Unlike my own record-beater where I omitted to record the second hand, the fastest time across the Atlantic still stands at 2 hours, 52 minutes and 59 seconds in 1996 by Captain Leslie Scott. This was preceded by a New York to London flight captained by Norman Britton who, in April 1990, managed 2 hours, 54 minutes and 30 seconds. These world records were helped by the hand of nature, namely the strength of the Atlantic tailwinds which assisted considerably in shrinking the flight time from a west to east direction.

Concorde also once flew from Miami to London in 3 hours and 50 minutes but with only two passengers aboard (a saving of over 5 hours and 15 minutes on the subsonic route). When Black Monday hit the financial world in 1987 the aircraft flew back shortly afterwards from New York. There was one solitary passenger aboard (the others no doubt counting their financial losses) and on arrival his luggage had been lost. That took some explaining away by the BA ground staff, but no doubt the passenger had felt very privileged to have the aircraft to himself and the undivided attention of six cabin crew.

Working to such a high standard, not to mention altitude, had its rewards. When we finally landed in New York with a full complement of passengers we had all made a strong crew bond. There was relief that the service had gone smoothly, as it invariably did, and pride that each and every one of us had worked hard to make a success of the service. We were undoubtedly a small close-knit family.

The New York Stopover and Dinner with a Singing Legend

The ground crew who met the Concorde flight in New York were the nicest and friendliest bunch of Americans you could meet. They were always so genuinely pleased to see us, conscientious in their work and nothing was ever too much trouble for them.

Having cleared customs in John F. Kennedy Airport and collected our luggage, a crew coach would be waiting for us to take us into the city. Occasionally when we were feeling reckless we took the short helicopter flight from the airport into midtown Manhattan. That was always a fun way to enter the bustling city – and the quickest! On the coach we would relieve the boredom of the 'stop–start' drive in heavy traffic by guessing the time it would take for us to pass through the Lincoln Tunnel. Bets were placed, money parted with, and it was always amusing if the cabin crew beat the flight crew who regarded themselves as experts in this game.

The discussion then inevitably moved on to the rest of the day's arrangements. Where were the girls shopping? Where was the venue for lunch? Which bar were we heading for in the evening? You could always guarantee to meet the male crew members in the evening at some bar or other. A favourite was an Irish bar, Rosie O'Grady's, or, for the flight crew, the Triple Inn. On smarter occasions it would be the Rainbow Room, the Russian Tea Rooms or one of the many chic restaurants New York had to offer. There was always a member of the crew keen to go to the theatre, which we did quite often.

Having checked into the hotel in Manhattan and after a quick change, the girls would invariably meet up and shop for 4 or 5 hours. (I often wonder how we did it for that long, having just walked the Atlantic!) The city had so many attractions to visit. Shopping would be interspersed with a trip to an art gallery, a walk in Central Park and plenty of breaks for coffee in the numerous bars.

If the cruise ship the *QE2* was in port we invariably received an invitation via the flight crew to go aboard for drinks and lunch. Concorde did many charters with the *QE2*. Passengers would fly out to New York on Concorde and join the cruise ship for a five-day trip back to Southampton. I remember one female passenger with her husband who had been more than pleased and grateful to fly back. They had had one of the suites on the *QE2* on the higher deck. During a particularly bad crossing on this occasion the ship had been extremely lively in the Atlantic seas, with the result that she had spent the entire time in her cabin. The supersonic flight was a very welcome alternative as a means to return home.

Before the 10.30 a.m. flight back to London we would meet up for breakfast at the local coffee shop round the corner. It was a 'home from home' experience. The waitresses knew us all by name. They were typical flamboyant New Yorkers and many a time they would regale us with their hilarious stories about their love lives. Similarly, they would know quite a bit about the domestic lives of the crew members. I'm sure they must have guessed about the various crew affairs as there were the regular couples who always flew together and that was surely no coincidence.

The nightlife in New York started early, which suited us well having flown to a 4-hour time change. Some of the bars in town would be heaving by 6.30 in the evening, discos and dancing in full flow. It was an eye-opening insight into New York City life. The city workers would flock to the bars, enjoy partying and be out in time for their commuter trains to take them home at a decent hour. It epitomised the Americans' way of life – they are known for working hard and partying hard, and we certainly took full advantage of it.

One of my most unforgettable evenings in New York was spent with the singer John Denver. Returning to New York on Concorde after a concert in London, he asked to visit the flight deck and he was up there for quite some time. As he was missing the dinner service I popped my head into the flight deck to see if he would like to eat. He was sitting in the left-hand seat, no doubt having a crash course in the myriad dials in front of him. John was a qualified pilot and so was totally absorbed and intrigued by the technology in front of him. I confess that in the dimmed light of the flight deck, our eyes met. It was one of those moments when the heart strings pull and you just know the chemistry is there. Later on he signed a menu for me and wrote, 'Sally, you have a lovely smile. Peace, John Denver'.

Later we got chatting and he asked me if I flew into New York very often. 'About once a week on average,' I replied. 'Sometimes twice.' He gave me one of his charismatic smiles and asked when I was going to be over next. Quite by chance our dates for being in New York coincided and, to my surprise, he asked if I would have dinner with him. The reply was naturally affirmative.

Two weeks later, I was bound for New York to meet up with my special date. Nature, however, was to play a bad card by producing a very stormy night and things were not about to run smoothly. We approached New York in the middle of a mighty rainstorm that made landing impossible. We were diverted to Newark. This had never happened to me before, nor would it ever again, but on this night of all nights fate stepped in.

Concorde made a bumpy approach through heavy rain clouds into Newark. We disembarked the passengers and waited. The captain, aware of my date as were all the crew, disappeared off to the operations room to sort out transport into the city and also to ask if John Denver's private jet had landed. He returned to the waiting crew who were as anxious as I was to know the outcome. Yes, his plane had landed at 4 p.m. that afternoon before the rainstorm. The captain was wonderfully sympathetic and asked for a coach to be sent as soon as possible. However, the journey still took 2½ hours. The New York skyline looked bleak and the coach trip seemed to take forever. We munched disconsolately on cheese rolls and drank brandy to warm ourselves up. It was around 9 p.m. when we finally checked into the hotel.

I had by this time given up all hope of seeing John for dinner. At the hotel check-in desk there were two messages to say Mr Denver had called. The crew were full of sympathy for my missed opportunity. Feeling pretty low, I went up to my room and resolutely took off my make-up, got undressed and slipped into bed. By this time it was 9.30 p.m. (1.30 a.m. UK time) and any chance of another call from John seemed out of the question. Superstars are probably not used to being stood up!

Having made myself comfortable between the sheets I was startled when the phone rang. True to his word, John was determined to keep the date. He told me that he and some friends were in a Japanese restaurant on the Upper West Side and would I be up to joining them? If there was a record time for a female getting showered, dressed and make-up on, I would most certainly have made the record book! Half an hour later, outwardly calm and composed but adrenalin bursting in my chest, I walked into the restaurant where John, with four of his male friends, gave me a very warm welcome. We drank sake and ate sushi and the weariness of the flight and delay evaporated as I got to know more about this amazing man.

We carried on drinking in a bar across the road. So absorbed were we in each other we hardly noticed the others leaving. There were crayons and paper covering the tables. John drew a big smiley face and wrote my name underneath it. We talked about his farm, his love of the wild open spaces, the Rockies being his favourite wilderness, and I became totally absorbed by him. He spoke passionately of wanting to be one of the first 'ordinary' men in space. He was firmly committed to the idea. He spoke vehemently about hunger in the world and was resolute about finding solutions to this. We discussed his concerts and his songwriting.

'How do feel when you walk out on stage in front of a vast audience like the Albert Hall and there's just you and your guitar?' I asked.

He smiled one of his enigmatic smiles. 'Just great, Sally,' he said. 'I love singing to the world whether it's two or 2,000.'

One subject that we didn't broach was his love life. He had divorced the year before. He was, however, very enthusiastic about his young daughter Jesse Belle, whom he had come to visit in New York. 'You must come and meet her,' he said 'Come over for a weekend.'

He was, without doubt, the most unpretentious star I have ever met. His million megawatt smile and absolute enthusiasm for life would 'fill a room', as they say. It was infectious and despite all his stardom he made you feel very special. Leaving the bar we stepped into his long, black stretch limo and headed off to the appropriately named Sally's Bar opposite the crew hotel. By this time it was late and the bar was quiet. He dismissed his driver and we sat drinking coffee and reflecting on life. Finally we walked back to my hotel and, stepping into the lift, we wondered when we would see each other again. The electricity between us would have driven that lift up to the twenty-third floor on its own. I knew I was going to find it hard to say goodnight, and as we stood outside the door to my room he asked if he could come in.

As tempted as I was, the reality of getting up in a few hours to work back to London was very much in the back of my mind, and I felt pretty sure that after the fabulous evening we would see each other again. I often reflect on this decision and still have this image in my mind of John walking back to his hotel in Central Park in the rain, at 3 in the morning. I fell asleep wondering about what might have been ...

The phone rang the next morning as I was getting ready for crew pick-up. It was John to say how much he enjoyed the evening and he hoped we might see each other again. We must not let distance come between us, he insisted. He gave me his address and phone number in Colorado. In the hotel lobby the crew were waiting for me and desperate to hear of the night's developments. I think I could have flown home under my own steam that day I was so elated.

John died in 1997 at the age of 53 as the result of an air crash. The small plane he was flying solo was new to him and the official report was that the fatal crash off the coast at Monterey, California, was pilot error. He was, however, an extremely experienced pilot. In his huge contribution to music he was the fourth highest selling American solo artist of all time, the others being Elvis Presley, Michael Jackson and Frank Sinatra. He left a legacy of hauntingly beautiful music, magical words and, for one lady, the memories of a beautiful night in rainy New York.

Naturally, as Concorde cabin crew we met many handsome, wealthy and *unavailable* men. They wore Saville Row suits and becoming smiles. There was always the odd one or two who were persistent in asking for our phone numbers. One of my regular passengers was a very highly educated Indian shipping magnate. He was always very charming and he invited me for dinner in a top London Indian restaurant. I remember quite clearly the drinks order consisted of three different types of bottled water. I don't remember being asked if I would like a glass of wine!

Then there was Tom, a very suave New Yorker with Paul Newman eyes. We had dinner in New York on several occasions. He knew all the best restaurants and treated me royally. One evening we ended up at a small café – the Lone Star Café. I was thrilled when we walked in to find one of my favourite singers, Don McLean, was playing. We stayed to hear him play his memorable numbers 'Vincent' and 'Starry, Starry Night'.

There were other stewardesses who dated famous people. A stewardess friend of mine was elated when she had met Eric Clapton on a flight and he asked for her phone number. Was this to be another 'nearly, not quite' moment, as happened so many times in our job? We all wanted to be the first to be updated on the progress report of Mr Clapton's dating. Meeting up with Annie over the next few days, the burning question was 'had she gone out on date with him?' She was mortified that he had rung twice when she had been out and left two messages. If mobile phone development had progressed a few years ahead of time who knows what might have happened?

One of my flying girlfriends befriended a passenger who always took her to Flushing Meadow to watch the international tennis tournaments. He was also very generous when he came to London and lent her his Rolls-Royce with a chauffeur. We enjoyed a very hedonistic shopping trip in London with our obliging chauffeur. There were, however, very few steward-esses who met the man of their dreams on these flights *and* managed to marry him! Mostly we were all dating boyfriends at home and as mine was involved with the Grand Prix world that again was another glamorous lifestyle.

CONCORDE CHARTERS AND A GOOD EXCUSE TO DISPLAY CONCORDE'S FLYING ABILITIES

Long-serving stewardess Jeannette Hartley became the first person to charter Concorde for a group of friends in 1981. Jeannette, who joined Concorde in 1977 and has an impressive record of 744 Atlantic crossings in twenty years, is a member of the Naval Reserve. Her colleagues there had often spoken of the desire to fly supersonic and Jeannette approached Concorde charters and a price was agreed to charter the aircraft. For 1 hour and 15 minutes' flight around the Bay of Biscay, British Airways agreed to charge £20,000. However, to Jeannette's disappointment, only eleven people came forward to take the flight even though the cost had been reduced to £17,500. At the time she was being interviewed by a woman's magazine and British Airways public relations department decided to seize on this to market her idea and the following day the *Daily Mail* published a picture of her standing in front of Concorde promoting her charter idea.

In three weeks Jeannette had filled not only one but two Concordes for her charter flight. Readers who had seen the opportunity of flying supersonic for £175 wasted no time in getting in touch with her. Jeannette told me, 'I was inundated with cheques. Letters would come through the post addressed to Ms Jeannette Hartley, Concorde Stewardess, Wexham, Bucks.' They all found their way to her house and

Jeannette Hartley's first charter with British Airways in 1981 around the Bay of Biscay. (Courtesy of Jeannette Hartley)

Jeannette admits she could have filled another Concorde. After that, the round the Bay of Biscay charters really took off.

Over the years we flew many charters. These charters were the saviours of Concorde's accounts and became very popular with Concorde fans due to their affordability. Some were brief 2-hour flights over the Bay of Biscay, giving our guests the experience of flying supersonic with a glass of champagne in hand. Others were of a longer duration. The first-timers on the charters were always so enthusiastic, as were the children who were lucky enough to be included. It was a pleasure to see their faces as they first stepped aboard, many speechless with excitement. During these short trips the emphasis was more on the performance of the aircraft than the in-flight service.

After serving lunch to our charter passengers we regarded ourselves lucky if we got any of the cutlery, china or glassware back. Everything that bore the Concorde logo was regarded as fair game by the passengers and some would take as much as they thought they could get away with as a memento of their flight. Most charter passengers had saved for a long time for their flight of a lifetime and they made sure they got their money's worth. Certificates signed by the crew and captain were also part of the package. An even greater delight was the invitation by the crew to visit the flight deck that, understandably, no passenger refused.

One of the memorable charters was to the RAF base at Mildenhall in Suffolk. We landed to see thousands of spectators lining the fencing alongside the runway to watch our arrival. However, Concorde was not the only highlight of the day. The Red Arrows display team was also there along with the American aerobatics team, the Vulcan bomber and the sinister Blackbird (also capable of flying supersonic, but at Mach 3 and at an altitude of 85,000ft).

The Red Arrows display from our vantage point was pretty unique – standing on the wings of the parked Concorde. We had removed our shoes and stepped out onto the long curved wing from one of the aircraft doors. Undoubtedly we had a good view, as the men in their magnificent flying machines never failed to impress. It was quite a bizarre experience too, seeing them flying in the Concorde formation from our unique position.

After watching this gravity defying display, we went to meet the pilots as they parked their nine aircraft close to ours. I was naively taken aback that as they stepped out of their cockpits they were as cool and relaxed as if they had just stepped off a bus! Not only were we in total awe of the pilots' flying prowess but it did not go unnoticed by the girls that they were all exceptionally good-looking, charming and very easy to talk to.

It was our turn next to impress the crowds. The 100 passengers who had paid for an hour's charter eagerly embarked Concorde for a 'spin round the bay'. Now, whether the 'jump jockeys' on the flight deck were trying to emulate the Red Arrows is debatable. Whether it was the fact that the aircraft was very light, having no baggage in the hold, but the 'boys at the front' were more than ready to show off their flying skills as well as the performance of Concorde. Our guests for the trip, grannies and youngsters alike, were excitedly awaiting the take-off. Concorde raced down the runway and headed up into the skies. There was huge G-force and the captain proudly announced that we had just climbed 11,000ft per minute. My stomach certainly felt like it had done just that.

Further aerobatics were in store. We headed out over the North Sea and then turned to approach the runway at the airbase. Beautiful to watch from the ground, no doubt, the captain did a superb approach, wheels skimmed the runaway with great precision and then we were off again climbing as fast as we had done the first time. We banked over and headed out to reach Mach 1. I have never been a lover of fairground rides and this was one I definitely wanted to get off.

Some of the passengers did not respond well either and I'm sure they had not been expecting to be part of such a heart stopping air display. Many delivered their champagne and snacks back into sick bags. Others were probably of the opinion the aircraft performed in this way all the time. I was moved to comment to the flight crew that the severity of the climb was indeed a first for me, and being an experienced flyer even I had found it a nauseating one. Sitting in their flight deck seats, beaming from ear to ear and no doubt immensely proud of themselves, the two pilots proudly announced they had given a superb display and it wasn't often they had the chance to fly such a lightweight Concorde and therefore show off its true performance levels … Mischievous boys let loose in a fairground!

On another occasion Concorde was flying in formation with another two Concordes at an air show. There were no passengers on this particular flight so the two stewardesses were standing idly in the front galley next to the flight deck, the door of which happened to be open. Now one of the stewardesses was well known as being extraordinarily verbose and was never short of words. The two girls were carrying on an avid conversation obviously unconcerned about the pretty crucial flying going on a few feet away from them. From the flight deck came a sharp retort from the captain. 'Will you two parakeets shut up? I'm trying to fly in formation!'

Concorde had flown several times with the Red Arrows at air displays. On one occasion Julia van den Bosch, our longest-serving supersonic stewardess, recalled the event:

> The captain wanted to stay as close to the Red Arrows as aviation law would permit. He also wanted to show Concorde off to the crowds below. Not to be left out of the Red Arrows consummate display he in turn performed a few aerobatics as part of the display. Unfortunately for the passengers this meant fighting off queasy stomachs and the laws of gravity.

Julia recalls that the view from the flight deck was amazing as they followed in the wake of such a highly experienced flying team, and she comments that this was a typical example of how working on Concorde made it so unlike any other aircraft. 'On which aircraft,' she commented, 'would your day's work include flying in formation with the Red Arrows in front of thousands of avid and enthralled fans?'

In 1986 Concorde was specially chartered to a group of Americans from New York's John F. Kennedy Airport. A hundred Americans had paid for the privilege of getting as close to one of Halley's Comet's rare appearances as humanly possible. It was, at the time, passing close to the earth and had not been seen since 1901. After several glasses of champagne the Americans were really getting excited at seeing this very rare spectacle in the sky.

Finally the captain announced that we would be passing the comet on the left-hand side but that he would be turning the aircraft so that the passengers on the right could have an equally good view. However, overexcited at glimpsing the comet there was a mad rush of passengers from the right-hand side to get a look at it. We had to announce that it was best if everyone remained in their seats. Champagne-fuelled as they were, there was a distinct reluctance to comply with this. The scientists had reported that this was a very bad year for seeing the comet and that it could only be seen with a telescope. Whether we saw it for sure is still open for debate, but our enthusiastic guests had a great time anyway.

The Red Arrows through the Concorde cockpit window. (Courtesy of Mike Bannister)

THE VIENNA BALL

One of the more glamorous annual charters was to fly 100 passengers to Vienna for the New Year's Eve Ball at the Hofburg
Imperial Palace. This event was the grand successor to the
Imperial Ball and the palace was home to the great Hapsburg
family. It was undeniably a great sense of occasion and a very
glittering way to see in the New Year.

Ball gowns and dinner suits were packed as most of the
crew had agreed to attend the ball. Having flown into Vienna
the day before we had a wonderful day exploring the city and
its wine bars. I had by this time met my husband who worked
on Concorde as a cabin service director and we were lucky
enough to have been rostered for this trip together. However,
our waltzing was twenty years out of practise so my husband
and I spent some time in the afternoon in our hotel room
going through the steps of the Viennese waltz.

Feeling very privileged to be at such an event, we drew up
in taxis in front of the palace feeling very much the part in our
long ball gowns and the men in their dinner suits. Our first
sight of the Hofburg Palace was memorable and as we entered
the interior we were even more taken aback at the grandeur.
At the top of the ornately decorated sweeping staircase were
two enormous arrangements of pink roses. Next to these were
two very large busts on plinths of two of the male Hapsburg
dynasty. To our amazement, one of the Hapsburg family members was there to greet us. Wearing a long white dress, this
vision of beauty looked like a princess – as she probably was.
The night was magical and we took to the floor to dance to the
magnificent orchestra playing the Viennese waltzes.

We weren't the only novice dancers on the dance floor that night, but it was such a grand setting few noticed the occasional wrong-footed step. As we returned to the hotel just after midnight, the sky was ablaze with fireworks that lit up the city. In the park opposite, the revellers went on until the early hours of the morning. The Viennese certainly know how to bring in the New Year.

The next evening we were scheduled to fly back to London. The passengers had experienced a wonderful New Year and were now quite weary after all the celebrations. No sooner had we taken off than the crew were aware that something was amiss. One of the stewardesses was hastily summoned to the flight deck. As she came back into the cabin, her face, as pale as an ostrich egg, registered shock. A light on the engineer's panel had shown that there was smoke in the aircraft hold and the possibility of a fire.

Barrie, the cabin service director who had been at the rear of the aircraft at the time, was also summoned to the captain and was told that we would have to return to Vienna with the possibility of a full passenger evacuation. In the meantime, the stewardess, who was still looking like she had seen the end of the world coming, and not wanting to let the standards slip even in an emergency, immediately went to the hat rack, found her hat and put it on.

'Why are you doing that?' questioned one of her colleagues.

'Well, if we have to evacuate the aircraft in a hurry at least I am correctly dressed for it.' Even with the prospect of an emergency situation our colleague was more than ready to look every inch the Concorde stewardess as she took on her role directing passengers down the slide and off the aircraft.

Following a jettisoning of fuel to lighten the landing weight, our Concorde was met by a fleet of fire engines and emergency vehicles, their lights pulsating in the darkness. It was soon established that this warning light had in fact had a

The Concorde charter to the New Year Vienna Ball at the Hofburg Palace; guests being greeted by a member of the Hapsburg family.

The grand entrance to the Hofburg Palace.

faulty reading, but nonetheless it had to be rectified before we could leave again for London. Our departure was thus delayed by a couple of hours until the problem was fixed. It was a salutary reminder that our much loved aircraft was not infallible and even she would pick her untimely moments to have the odd malfunction.

Another potential safety concern occurred to this same stewardess when she was working in the front galley on another flight. As you can imagine, one of the responsibilities of a stewardess is to have a heightened awareness of any unfamiliar noise that might be heard whilst in the cabin. My colleague was instantly alerted when she heard a buzzing noise emanating from the flight deck. This was not a sound she could identify and her first thoughts were that it was an emergency signal emanating from one of the instruments. Apprehensively, she ventured into the flight deck not sure what to expect. However, to her surprise the sound was no more than an electric shaver and she was greeted by the captain having a shave. So much for strange noises!

ROUND-THE-WORLD
CHARTERS AND ONE
FOR OPERA LOVERS

The 'Round-the-World' charters became a successful money earner for Concorde and must have surely been the ultimate experience for the flying enthusiast.

In 1988 Imperial Tobacco sponsored a thirteen-day trip for competition winners of their John Player Special brand of cigarette. This was quite a unique charter as some of the passengers had never flown before. Finding themselves with a round-the-world ticket flying supersonic must have been mind-blowing and, in some cases, quite a daunting prospect for these first-timers. These were ordinary working folk who suddenly found themselves on a holiday of a lifetime and about to embark on a trip they would only have previously dreamt about.

The flight left London via New York. Their next stopover was San Francisco for a couple of nights, then on to Honolulu where everyone was met with the traditional welcome of a colourful flower lei. Even Concorde was included and had one draped across her nose. Guam, an island in the Pacific, was next on the stopover. Not since Captain Cook landed in 1778 had an arrival caused such a stir as thousands turned out to watch Concorde's arrival. From Guam on to Hong Kong, then to Bali, Colombo and Bahrain; it was a trip of a lifetime for those lucky enough to be on it and for the fortunate crew.

In 1989 another charter took place with an American company. As the passengers were elderly there was also a doctor on board. The passengers were all from the southern states of America, very much 'old money' and very charming and gracious. Dee Bull, a fellow stewardess, takes up the story:

Originally we were to position to Hong Kong and work back to Delhi the next day. However, it was decided the crew should be there for the handing over of the departing crew so we had in fact arrived a day early to attend a cocktail party. We then had five days off whilst our passengers were flown up to Beijing with a Chinese carrier [Concorde was not allowed to go there].

So we started the trip well rested (although as ex-short-haul crew we rushed around Hong Kong trying to fit in all the sightseeing and shopping, including a boat trip to Macau for the day).

The catering and wines on Concorde were superb. The only instruction we were given when we left London was that at the end of each sector, all wine was to be 'disposed of' as we would have new provisioning for the next sector – it was difficult to know how to dispose of it. However, an economic solution from the crew was reached!

Wherever we arrived we were met with chaotic scenes as the station managers were eager to impress friends and guests with a tour of Concorde. As soon as all our passengers had disembarked our wonderful captain, Chris McMahon, gave the order that no one was to be allowed onto the aircraft for 15 minutes. The flights were pretty hard work, so it was wonderful to just sit and relax with a little of what had to be 'disposed of'!

In Delhi we flew up to the Taj Mahal with our guests on Air India. They were staying overnight in order to see the breathtaking sight of the Taj at sunset and dawn. We, however, had to get back for the next leg of the trip the following morning so we had to take our life in our hands and endure the death-defying taxi ride back to Delhi.

Whilst at the Taj Mahal, one of the stewardesses, Margaret, slipped and sprained her ankle. The doctor strapped it up but she was very anxious not to be left behind. Help was at hand in the guise of the 'PR' pilot, Dick, who had worked as cabin crew when the company had decommissioned Trident aircraft and were overstaffed with first officers. Dick volunteered to work in the cabin. The passengers were told of Margaret's accident and Dick, the 'new recruit', became a firm favourite in the cabin.

We flew on to Cairo and our first day included a visit to the museums and 'Son et Lumiere' at the pyramids. Our final evening was one of mystery and exotic Arabian hospitality at its best. Wearing the traditional dress of 'dish dashes' we were taken out to the pyramids. Imagine the scene amongst the backdrop of one of the greatest wonders of the world. As we approached a huge Bedouin tent, we were greeted by riders on magnificent dancing horses carrying large flares to guide us in. It was a magical evening.

The world's best belly dancer was there with swirling dervishes and a magnificent meal was laid on for us. (There was even a whole roast lamb on a spit outside, and I remember going out into the dark night and seeing only the outline of the pyramids in front of me, and having to pinch myself that I was actually getting paid for this!)

One of the ladies on board I particularly recall was elegant and must have been in her eighties. She had porcelain skin and in her gloved hands she smoked a cigarette with a cigarette holder. She had to have a wheelchair. Whilst her husband was disembarking with the hand baggage, I heard her say to him in a strong, deep southern drawl, 'You be careful there, honey'.

'Don't you worry about me' he replied.

To which she replied, 'I ain't worried about you, I'm worried about your pacemaker!'

Sadly when we got back, despite taking all precautions I went down with salmonella, I guess it was a hazard of the job. No one else did, so it was just bad luck on my part.

Concorde taking off. (Courtesy of Peter March)

Another distinctive shot of Concorde taking off, showing the vortex effect on the wing. (Courtesy of Peter March)

Concorde climbing, showing the afterburners. (Courtesy of Peter March)

Concorde nose. (Shutterstock, Image ID: 2922876. Copyright: Kevin)

The distinctive nose cone of the supersonic aircraft. Concorde shot from beneath. (Shutterstock, Image ID: 224094943. Copyright: af8images)

Concorde at Singapore. (Courtesy of Mike Bannister)

The leather seating inside Concorde. (Shutterstock, Image ID: 162863810. Copyright: Marbury)

The curvature of the earth. (Courtesy of Mike Bannister)

The captain's view. (Courtesy of Mike Bannister)

The pilots' panel. (Courtesy of Mike Bannister)

Sally and crew on location.

The Mildenhall Air Show, Suffolk, with the crew standing on Concorde's wing watching the Red Arrows in Concorde formation in 1983.

The crew, including senior pilot Jock Lowe and Dick Bell (cabin service director), at Mildenhall Air Show with the Red Arrows.

A Concorde unscheduled service to Glasgow. We were met with the red carpet and bagpipes, a true Scottish welcome!

A round-the-world charter in Honolulu.

Fred Finn in front of his beloved Concorde.

Concorde presentation, 10 March 2001, after refurbishment of aircraft prior to its re-entry into service. (Courtesy of Louise Brown)

Concorde in her final livery. (Courtesy of Mike Bannister)

The last flight was an emotional experience. (Courtesy of Julia van den Bosch)

In the mid-eighties Concorde was chartered to fly to Luxor in Egypt. A hundred opera fans had booked to experience Verdi's famous opera *Aida* in the unique setting of the 3,500-year-old Luxor Temple. Placido Domingo topped the bill with a cast of 1,500 singers, dancers, musicians and extras and even a lion. It was estimated that 30,000 people in total attended the opera, including sixty European princes and princesses.

Regrettably, although we were not far from the venue, we failed to get tickets for the opera. Our accommodation was a Nile riverboat with a view across to the Valley of the Kings and this made an interesting interlude from the normal five-star city hotels we stayed in. The next morning, determined to enjoy the Nile experience, a group of us visited the Karnak Temple, the most visited site after the pyramids at Giza. Its size and preservation was quite awe inspiring.

A trip to Egypt would not have been true to form if some-one had not gone down with a serious stomach bug. Sadly, on our return to London, it was one of our female passengers who had to be stretchered off.

Another incident aboard involved one high-ranking, opera-loving cabinet minister. Prior to landing we were giving out boxed models of Concorde as a keepsake of the flight. Most passengers were very appreciative of their 'gift'. Not so the min-ister, who abruptly told the stewardess, '*Why* would *I* want one of these?' and handed it back to her. She was visibly upset by his unwarranted rudeness. The watchword in situations like these was to 'keep smiling'. Sometimes it wasn't as easy as you imagine.

It was always company policy that each Concorde pas-senger received a gift at the end of the flight. These varied greatly from grey leather bridge sets to leather hip flasks, silver drinks labels, Concorde leather gift tags, pens, diaries, notebooks, writing pads, scarves and ties, to name but a few. No doubt these are now amongst some of the passengers' prized possessions.

There was always one who wanted to take an extra souvenir home with them. I think the most audacious request I recall was when a passenger very seriously asked me if he could have a dozen of the miniature salt and pepper sets for his dining table at home. 'They would be quite unique wouldn't they?' he suggested. I couldn't disagree with him, could I?

PROMOTING CONCORDE: UNIQUE TIMES AND A TRIP TO DETROIT

One of the tasks of the Concorde fleet, as flagship to British Airways, was to be involved in promotional work. Detroit was one of the destinations, no doubt to impress our American cousins who had slowly come round to the 'noisy' supersonic aircraft.

It was a memorable trip, not least because we flew an empty Concorde over there. To sit in one of the passenger seats with no work to do gave the flight an added exclusivity and made a pleasant change from working across the Atlantic. One of the stewards served us lunch and that even further enhanced the hedonistic experience. It was the only time I ever flew passenger on Concorde and got paid for it.

Our first stopover was New York. From there two Concordes were to fly to Detroit and land on parallel runways. Captain John Hutchinson was flying one and the other, which I was on, was captained by Colin Morris. It had been decided that John's Concorde would taxi out first at JFK followed by ours. Now, whether there was a competitive spirit between these two captains, or Colin Morris just wanted to have a joke with John, I'm not sure, but it was very amusing when Colin jumped the queue and we arrived at the departure runway first. There was a great deal of friendly bickering over the airwaves. Colin wanted to be the first to arrive in the Detroit area.

As it happened, both aircraft arrived there at the same time. One by one we did a planned overshoot at 200ft and then came around to land simultaneously on parallel runways. It was an unforgettable flying moment as both captains did a superb job and the two aircraft landed perfectly together. It was certainly a novel experience to look across at the other runway and see another Concorde landing at the same time.

A crowd of 20,000 spectators had gathered to watch the display. The control tower relayed to the flight crew that they had never seen such spectacular flying. In the airport manager's lounge there was quite a reception waiting for us as TV and press were there, as well as VIPs and members of the airline's executive management. We felt quite the celebrities and after that spectacular arrival we were as jubilant as the crowds who had watched our arrival.

Captain Morris volunteered me to be interviewed by one of the TV stations. Thus the job of stewardess widened its horizons and I found my 15 minutes of fame on live TV. One of the questions I was asked was if one experienced jet lag on the Atlantic crossings. Momentarily I hesitated. I think I might have been in trouble with the company if I had said yes. The theory behind such short flying times is that there is no jet lag and certainly from the passengers' point of view I had never heard of them suffering from it. Even 'three times across the Atlantic in one day' Richard Noble, in his record-breaking event, commented that he had no jet lag.

The curious observation about working on Concorde was that for the first six months all the crews were absolutely fine and the newcomers who had left long haul were delighted that this was one of the bonuses of flying supersonic. There was no great mix of time changes. On long haul one could be in Tokyo one week, San Francisco the next and Sydney the following week. The body clock could become very scrambled. However, on Concorde, large numbers of us agreed that after approximately six months of supersonic flying a form of tiredness equivalent to jet lag hit our systems. The flight deck never had a problem but for those of us making two trips to New York a week, it most definitely had an effect.

After the American press had taken photographs for the local newspapers and the TV stations had had their fill of interviews we left the welcoming reception to watch the two Concordes depart for London, again with a spectacular display. Taking off pretty much one after the other, they climbed into the skies then returned, banking overhead before starting their supersonic climb across the Atlantic. We all cheered and waved and our hearts swelled with pride at such superlative flying. Along with the Red Arrows, Concorde was an icon of aviation and made us all justly proud to be British.

That night there were two Concorde crews remaining and we were all in full party mode. The airport authorities had laid on a fantastic party for us and we all felt very fortunate to have been part of a landmark in history-making. One of the comments from the airport managers was that we all seemed to be a very close and friendly group. And that's how it was. We felt immensely privileged to work on such a fleet.

With all the official duties over and enjoying the ample American hospitality we did let our hair down a little. One of the sillier moments of the evening was my introduction to a game called 'Dead Ants'. There were seven of us, flight crew included, in the lift descending to the ground floor for the party. When one of the crew called 'dead ants' we all had to fall onto the floor and act dead. Unfortunately at this moment the lift arrived at its destination and to the amazement of the couple standing at the open doors there were seven of us giggling and sprawled on the floor. Thank goodness they hadn't recognised the captain and first officer out of uniform.

The trip finished in suitable style when we flew back to London first class on a British Airways 747. 'A long way to go for a party', I wrote in my diary.

BARBADOS BOUND

The first scheduled Concorde flights to Barbados began in February 1984 and the incoming crew on this inaugural flight were treated royally and invited to a champagne reception at the governor general's residence.

I was scheduled to fly the return flight to London. We had flown out on Concorde to New York the previous day and were booked on a passenger flight to Barbados on British West Indian Airlines. Leaving a cold, stony-grey New York and finding ourselves in the warmth of the Caribbean was indeed a winter's tonic and a wonderful break from working out of London.

During my years flying on 747s I had spent many holidays visiting Barbados. Being such a regular it was like a homecoming to be staying on the island again where I had many friends. Our schedule included a day off and the next day proved to be a lovely break from work as the whole crew chartered a catamaran and we sailed along the beautiful coastline, sampling the rum punch that was liberally served to us by our Caribbean friends of long standing.

Sunset is always a magical time in the Caribbean and it is the one place in the world I have visited where people gather on the beach to witness the ending of the day, locals and tourists alike. It is truly a moment of tranquility as the sun slips behind the skyline and it gives one a moment for reflection and gratitude at being in such a heavenly place. And there were many happy memories of being there.

Luciano Pavarotti loved to holiday in Barbados and in the nineties he flew out on Concorde and stayed at the Sandy Lane Hotel. On one occasion, my husband and I were there with our 4-year-old son. It was a glorious morning and we were taking a very early stroll along the Sandy Lane beach (my young son liked to rise early, whichever time zone he was in). Standing in the sea was this larger than life figure, Pavarotti, with his Italian secretary/girlfriend, Nicoletta, whom he later married in 2003. As my son looked across to him, Pavarotti began to sing in his wonderfully sonorous voice, 'Good Morning Good Morning'. I don't think my son was fully aware that he had just been serenaded by one of the world's greatest living legends in opera.

With the commencement of the Concorde service, the morning after our arrival was business as usual. We enjoyed a relaxed hotel breakfast in the sunshine and it was a very pleasant thought that all the crew seated around the table were really looking forward to going to work.

At 10 a.m. precisely we joined officials and VIPs at the Grantley Adams Airport waiting for Concorde's final approach into Barbados. There was a wonderful atmosphere. Crowds had gathered on the viewing galleries and rooftops of the terminal. A steel band dressed in green and yellow was playing at full volume as a warm breeze wafted over us. We spotted the first glimpse of the silver-winged bird as it approached from out of a clear blue sky. Glinting in the sunlight, it throttled back to pass overhead, and turned up the coastline before finally coming into land. With its familiar poise for landing, stick legs protruding down and droop nose, it was like a much-loved family pet that, as soon as one saw it, one's heart lurched.

Officials stepped onto the tarmac to greet the passengers and crew. There were smiles all round, especially from the passengers who probably were still in shock that the 'bird' they were emerging from had delivered them from London in 3 hours and 30 minutes, less than half the flying time of the subsonic jets. Breakfast before leaving home and an afternoon dip in the Caribbean Sea was quite a good way to start a holiday!

As soon as we were allowed onto the aircraft to prepare for the return journey, we realised that patience was the order of the day. Stowing food and beverages on Concorde was a first for the Barbados catering crew. What they lacked in knowledge of the new stowing procedures they made up for in enthusiasm. It was a case of dealing with the unfamiliar, and teething problems were bound to happen. Despite the delay of getting everything on board, the local catering team was immensely proud to be a part of the supersonic experience.

Concorde operated a twice weekly service to Barbados throughout the winter and it was invariably full. It also carried many of the stars and celebrities who visited the island.

LIFE WITH THE SUPERSTARS, ROCK STARS AND MEGA STARS

If I had to name all the famous people I had met during my time on Concorde it would be an extremely long list of both household names and icons. They could be divided into categories of movie stars, rock stars, opera stars and sports stars, with a subcategory for rising stars, fading stars and ever-shining stars. But enough of the galaxy.

There were also thespians, movie producers, film directors, as well as bankers and business executives who were hot names in the finance world and who were regular commuters. There were chairmen of global companies, media barons, authors and no doubt mafia men and the odd criminal from the underworld.

Whatever their trade, whatever their talent, whatever their notoriety, good or bad, they were all treated the same. If you had a boarding pass for the pointy-nosed aircraft, you were treated like a star whether you were a pensioner who had spent your life savings on an hour round the bay, or a first-time flyer with no inkling of the finesse of the machine you were about to fly on.

On a few unscheduled occasions, British Airways management decided that instead of using the usual 737 for the early flight to Glasgow, they would lay on a Concorde, unknown to the passengers. This was a superb piece of advertising as the unexpected arrival of Concorde on a commuter run to Glasgow was quickly snatched up by the media and attracted a lot of TV coverage.

Most passengers were absolutely thrilled to have this rare experience thrust upon them. However, there were one or two, and I hope you know who you are out there, who walked on completely nonchalant and whose only concern was to know if the flight would arrive on time! I guess the equivalent would be if someone was catching a Number 9 bus to work and along came a stretch limo and chauffeur to take him to his destination. Wouldn't there be some acknowledgement of such a pleasant surprise? I can't imagine anyone not being in awe of the upgrade.

At Glasgow Airport we were greeted in true Scottish style by some extremely tall bagpipe players who, positioned at the bottom of the aircraft steps, played the passengers off the aircraft and across the tarmac – not a bad way to start a morning's work.

In the icon category of famous passengers, the American movie producer of the James Bond films, Cubby Broccoli, is one I remember well. He had enormous presence. Albert 'Cubby' Broccoli was born in Queens, New York City and in 1962 produced the first Bond movie, *Dr No*, with Harry Saltzman. They went on to make more successful Bond movies until they parted company in 1976. Cubby's last movie, *GoldenEye*, came out in 1995 and he died a year later. He was indeed an imposing character and I guess many a female 'wannabe' actor in my situation would have been in awe of meeting this famous person. They might even have grabbed the moment to try to get an introduction into the movie world.

However, I had no such aspirations as, several years earlier, I had been given a taster of movie making. I had flown into Toronto on a 747 trip and on our day off, myself and another stewardess went to a prestigious lakeside country club to relax and sunbathe. I guess this was a perk of the job that we had access to such establishments which cost the members dearly in annual fees. Having settled ourselves on sunbeds we did notice that there was unusual activity around us in the form of cameras, lighting and film crew. However, our attention was focused on chilling out and getting sun onto our pale winterised bodies. A while later, I was aware of a shadow standing over me and looked up to see one of the film crew looking at me. 'How would you like to be in a movie?' he asked. This was the director speaking.

My immediate answer was, 'I will have to call my agent first' (I did think he was joking). He smiled at my reply then asked, if I agreed to do it would I go to make-up and did I have any other clothes with me? As these offers don't come along every day, I disengaged myself from the comfortable lounger and followed the director to the film crew. Suddenly I was being treated quite royally. The guys did a lighting test on me, they patiently explained what I had to do (NOT look at the cameras) and after an hour of lights and cameras being positioned correctly we were ready to film. Then the male lead arrived whom I was to play opposite. I can't remember him engaging me in much conversation and it was down to work straight away.

I have to add at this point that I was a stand-in for the famous star, Kim Novak. Apparently I had the same length blonde hair and, as I was to be slightly off the main shot and it was only a back view, it didn't matter too much about the looks! The scene took a brief 5 minutes in which the male lead answered the phone at a table on the terrace overlooking the lake with me beside him. Was I paid for my time? No. Did I ever get to see the movie on screen? No. And probably, like all good pieces of film, my part ended up on the cutting room floor.

STARS OF STAGE AND SCREEN

In the movie mogul world, those who could be counted as 'regulars' were actor and film producer Sir Richard Attenborough and Michael Winner. They often sat together. A quiet, unassuming character was Jim Henson, creator of the Muppets, who died in 1990. The legendary director Steven Spielberg also flew on many occasions.

Barbra Streisand, who flew on it several times, was remembered for her comment that she believed the nose of Concorde was inspired by her own nose shape and therefore the aircraft should have been called 'the Streisand'. Lauren Bacall travelled with us and, despite having a reputation of being a tough cookie, Purser Julia van den Bosch recalls having a long heart to heart with her. Julia had just broken up with her boyfriend and Miss Bacall spent some time with her listening sympathetically. 'Keep busy' were her words of advice, which was not difficult to do in our job.

In the A-list film star category, Liz Taylor had to rank amongst the highest, along with Robert de Niro, Tom Cruise, Claudette Colbert, Ben Kingsley, Richard Dreyfuss, Peter Sellers and Michael Douglas, to name but a few. Sadly, some of those are no longer with us. Peter Sellers was accompanied by his actress wife, Lynne Frederick. After Peter Sellers' death in 1980 she went on to marry David Frost. This was dissolved a year later and she died at the age of 39 of substance abuse.

Sir Richard Harris, also now passed to the great heavenly Concorde 'check-in', was a regular and it was ironic that his normal persona of being a 'hell-raiser' and alcoholic was very much absent. As the flight progressed I found out why. He had given up drinking and turned vegetarian. Known for his famous role in *Camelot* and his award nomination for his role in *The Field*, he was also a poet, singer and performed in theatre. Latterly, his best remembered role was that of Dumbledore in the first two Harry Potter films. Sadly, this once flamboyant character died at the age of 72 in 2002 from Hodgkin's disease.

The late Bob Hope, comedian of great style, made the infamous comment when seeing the size of the Concorde toilet that it was no larger than a broom cupboard. 'Hey guys, you really have to decide what you're gonna do before going into one of these. Either reverse in, or forward for us guys.'

There was the elusive Rudolph Nureyev who confessed to the crew he was petrified of flying. He remained anonymous, wrapped up in a scarf and balaclava and immersed in his own fears for the whole flight. He died from AIDS in January 1993 at the young age of 54.

Another famous face who flew on Concorde was Grace Jones. On two occasions she boarded the aircraft wearing a floor length dark brown cloak with a hood (very Scottish Widows advert) that covered her face completely. She kept her face covered for the entire flight, neither eating nor drinking anything.

John F. Kennedy junior, the son of President John F. Kennedy and Jackie Kennedy, was on a Concorde flight a short while before he died in 1999. Julia van den Bosch, who was purser aboard the flight to New York, commented that not only was he incredibly good-looking but he oozed charisma and charm. He was 38 years old at the time of his death. He had been piloting a light aircraft off the coast of Martha's Vineyard, Massachusetts, when it crashed into the Atlantic Ocean. His wife, Carolyn Bessette, and sister-in-law, Lauren, were also on the flight. All three were killed.

Other famous celebrities who were pilots themselves always received an invitation to the flight deck. At the higher end of the pilots was Buzz Aldrin, one of the astronauts on the Apollo 11 mission to the moon in 1969. He was the second person to walk on the moon. He was made extremely welcome by the flight crew and I'm sure they had many stories to exchange about flying in space or on the edge of it. It is worthy of mention that there are more astronauts than Concorde pilots – a rare breed indeed.

Elizabeth Taylor was an icon I had always wanted to meet, and on the occasion she travelled with us it was undoubtedly a very special experience. She was between husbands at the time, having divorced American politician John Warner in 1982 and was yet to marry husband number eight, Larry Fortensky, in 1991. She boarded the aircraft with a male companion and sat at the rear of the front cabin. In the row across the aisle from her was Michael Douglas accompanied by a starlet.

As we taxied along the runway Miss Taylor was not in her seat. We found her holding the toilet door open and washing a cosmetic bag in the sink. When asked if she needed assistance she replied, 'No, its fine. I just spilt some make-up in my bag here.' And she obliged us by returning to her seat.

I was working in the rear cabin for the flight but was keen to have another look at the movie legend I had always admired. My girlfriend Bernadette, working in the front cabin, suggested I take the drink Miss Taylor had ordered to her. 'And just take a look at those violet eyes,' she added. It was one of those moments in one's career one never forgets – the first sight of those amazing eyes. And the beauty that had decorated the film screens during my impressionable years. Never as a teenager would I have imagined meeting her. Drink delivered, I returned to continue the drinks service.

On my way up to the front cabin later in the flight I passed Bernadette chatting to Miss Taylor. I paused, curiosity getting the better of me. 'May I say, Miss Taylor, your ring is absolutely stunning,' Bernadette was saying. I paused some more. Bernadette was no stranger to expensive jewellery; in fact, along with clothes and shoes, it could be counted as one of her passions in life. Miss Taylor appeared flattered.

'Well try it on, honey,' she said giving us both one of those intriguing smiles as she slipped the ring off her finger and handed it to Bernadette. This was the ring she wore almost daily for forty years. It was 33.19 carats and bought for her by her husband, Richard Burton. She removed it as casually as if it were a piece of insignificant costume jewellery.

'May we?' Bernadette asked pointing to the toilets.

'Sure, go take a look,' Miss Taylor replied, probably amused at the incredulity on our faces. Bernadette and I, ensconced in the privacy of the toilet, both tried on the ring, admiring its beauty in the mirror. What a moment to have such a beautiful diamond on one's finger, and belonging to such a movie legend. It was a pity that mobile phones with cameras were not on the market then. Having gloated over this enormous diamond we returned it to its owner. On Miss Taylor's death in 2011 the ring sold at auction for £5.6 million, surely the most expensive piece of jewellery that will ever sit on my finger!

As a mention, Miss Taylor was not averse to removing her rings to show them to other people. There was an even bigger 69-carat ring that Richard Burton had bought for her 40th birthday. Sitting next to Princess Margaret at a dinner party the princess commented that the ring was 'vulgar'. Miss Taylor offered it to her to try on, which the princess did. 'Not so vulgar now it's on your finger, is it Ma'am?' was her brave comment.

The iconic film star Claudette Colbert shared common ground with Elizabeth Taylor in that they both played Cleopatra. Miss Colbert's performance was in 1934, almost thirty years earlier than Miss Taylor's. When Concorde started its winter schedules to Barbados, Miss Colbert used this service to fly to her home on the west coast of the island. In the late thirties she was the highest paid Hollywood actress and co-starred with names such as Edward G. Robinson, John Wayne and Clark Gable. When I met her at the age of 82 she looked incredibly youthful. She told me she loved Barbados and owed her good health to the climate there. 'And this,' she said, pointing to her topped up glass of champagne. 'These two things keep me in good health.'

Another Concorde passenger and film star of the old movie era was Lillian Gish. She earned the title the 'First Lady' of American cinema and had a film career spanning seventy-five years. Her role in silent cinema is legendary and her last film was at the age of 93 in which she appeared with Bette Davis. She died in 1993, aged 99. For such a lady the experience of flying Concorde must have been truly memorable. As she told my flying colleague, Louise Brown, when she was born flying hadn't even been invented. She was 10 years old when the American Wright brothers took to the air in their flying machine.

High-profile film star Liza Minnelli had just married her agent, David Gest, when she flew on Concorde. She had, by all accounts, been very successful at a dramatic weight loss. During the breakfast service, she was about to accept a croissant from the bread basket. However, a halting hand from her husband reached across to stop her. Miss Minnelli did not argue the point and refused the temptation. A while later, however, she passed by the galley and asked for a croissant, which she ate with great relish. As a tribute to her attention to detail she did ask the crew member if there were any telltale crumbs around her mouth before returning to her seat and her watchful husband.

Concorde was, more than any other aircraft, a magnet for the rich and famous and it was interesting to see that even well-known stars were excited about flying on it. In the fashion world, Ralph Lauren and Gloria Vanderbilt commuted from New York to London. Estée Lauder, who co-founded the

American Estée Lauder cosmetics company with her husband, was a pleasure to meet. She was famous for her quote, 'There are no ugly women, only women who don't care or believe they're not attractive.' She was, without doubt, an amazing example of the excellence of her products. Her complexion was beautiful. I took it as a very Estée(med) compliment when she commented that I had a good complexion.

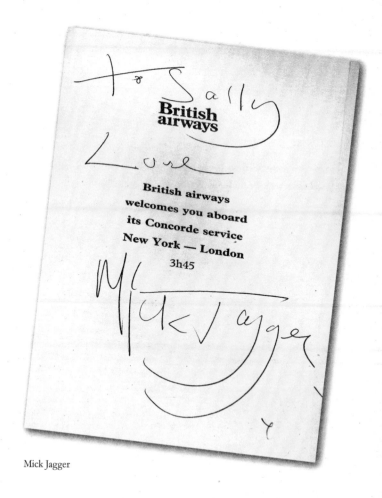

Mick Jagger

London—New York

3h55

Sally,
I think you have a
lovely smile
Peace.

BA 195 Con. I 11283

John Denver (courtesy of the author)

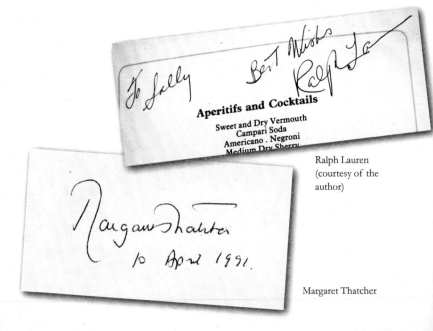

To Sally   Best Wishes   Ralph La

Aperitifs and Cocktails
Sweet and Dry Vermouth
Campari Soda
Americano . Negroni
Medium Dry Sherry

Ralph Lauren
(courtesy of the
author)

Margaret Thatcher
10 April 1991.

Margaret Thatcher

Paul McCartney

Lillian Gish

Robert de Niro
(courtesy of the
author)

Henry Kissinger

(Unless indicated, all courtesy of Louise Brown)

Lauren Bacall

Dolly Parton

John F. Kennedy (© NASA/KSC)

Sir Paul McCartney (© Richard Gunn)

Sir David Frost (© Chatham House)

Sir Richard Attenborough (© Gordon Correll)

Robin Gibb (© Robin Reigns/Wikimedia Commons)

Phil Collins

John Denver (© Liam White/Alamy)

Liz Taylor

Michael Jackson

John Travolta (© Towpilot/Wikimedia Commons)

ROCK STARS ON BOARD

Over the years, Concorde carried a fair selection of the world's top musicians – rock stars and classical stars alike. In the operatic world Placido Domingo, Luciano Pavarotti and Kiri Te Kanawa were all celebrities we had the pleasure of meeting (as they were regular passengers).

Boy George, the pop icon of the seventies and early eighties, was a colourful, friendly guy who was always expertly made up. When I met him he was travelling with his partner, male singer Marilyn. Before they boarded the flight from New York they had had a disagreement over something. This resulted in Marilyn sitting at the rear of the aircraft and Boy George in the front cabin. I was allotted to play messenger girl between the two in an attempt to sort out their differences. I obviously failed, as they got off in London still not talking!

Diana Ross travelled solo on occasions. Her huge wide tresses of hair were amazing. I was on one flight working with my husband who had flown with her quite recently. In fact, when she boarded the aircraft she addressed him by his first name – that really impressed the crew. Sadly, there was an incident prior to leaving London when she was taken off the aircraft by police for insulting a security officer. However, she still flew Concorde back to New York the following day.

Unlike today's high security where the flight crew are locked in the flight deck and have very little interaction with the passengers, in the 1980s any passenger who asked to see the flight deck was automatically invited up. When a name like Dolly Parton appeared on the passenger manifest the invitation from the captain was issued very smartly. I clearly remember the captain's beaming expression when we told him Dolly Parton was on board. 'Bring her up to see us,' he said enthusiastically.

The engineer and first officer were also very keen to meet her. After finishing her meal Dolly, looking every inch the glamorous star and as beautiful in the flesh as she appears in films and on TV with her waspish waist, stunning figure and a mass of blonde hair (a wig which she owns up to), sauntered up to see the 'boys in charge'. She was up there quite a while and I'm sure the conversation didn't exclusively revolve around the technicalities of flying. When Dolly emerged from the flight deck she gave us one of her radiant flirtatious smiles. 'Hey, I sure left those guys feeling horny,' she remarked, with a wink and in her deep southern drawl.

Robin Gibb first came on one of my flights with his personal assistant, Dwina. Robin was a strict vegetarian (like Sir Richard Harris) and special food was always put on for him. The second time I met them, Dwina was blossoming with pregnancy and the third time, Dwina was married and now to be addressed as Mrs Robin Gibb. It was interesting to note the different changes in circumstances with some of our regulars.

Like Robin, Barry Gibb flew regularly to Miami where both brothers had homes. Other singers who travelled with us were Ringo Starr with his wife Barbara Bach, and Paul McCartney. It was not unknown for Paul McCartney to pick up his guitar and sing in the aisles when he was married to Linda. On one occasion when steward Steve Whitehead was working on board, it was his birthday. Elton John was also on the aircraft and both he and Paul McCartney sang a duet to him.

Michael Jackson, unlike his public persona of being a very private individual, was very affable to the crew and passengers. Purser Julia van den Bosch recalls being nervous about asking for his autograph, but he was more than happy to sign menus for her and other fans on the flight. He was surprisingly interactive and he was a listening person, Julia recalls, a rare attribute amongst some of the superstars. Jackson met his untimely death in 2009, aged 50.

Whitney Houston's father, John Houston, travelled with us from New York to London at a time when his daughter was at the height of her career. He was her business manager and Whitney was on tour in Europe. Chatting to him after the meal service, I commented to him on what a talented daughter he had and how I loved her music. He thanked me and asked if I would like to see her in concert in London. Two tickets were arranged for collection at Wembley Stadium and my girlfriend and I had superb seats to watch the talented performer.

My husband, however, was unable to go as he was away at the time. Two weeks later, John Houston was on a flight returning from London to New York. He remembered me and asked if I enjoyed the concert. I enthused about it and thanked him profusely, adding that my husband was quite envious that he had missed it owing to his work schedule. Without a second's hesitation Mr Houston suggested, 'Why don't you take him to the next concert?' Whitney was performing in Germany and then returning to Wembley for the last part of the tour. Sure enough, John arranged tickets from the New York office and my husband and I were able to see her. It showed the caring and kindness of Whitney's gentle-natured father.

There were other occasions of generosity shown by the passengers. When the renowned chef Delia Smith flew to Barbados one Christmas she invited all the crew to lunch at the Royal Pavilion on Boxing Day. Similarly, Burton Race extended an invitation to all the crew to his Michelin-star restaurant in Berkshire.

Flying Concorde opened up so many opportunities, and in some places even just the word 'Concorde' worked the magic. Steward Steve Whitehead had flown in with the crew to New York for an overnight stopover. Learning that Frank Sinatra was appearing at Carnegie Hall that night he wasted no time in going down to the box office, a few blocks away from the hotel, to see if there were any tickets available.

Not unexpectedly, Steve was told the concert was a complete sell-out. Looking suitably disappointed, Steve said he had flown over on Concorde in the hope of seeing Frank Sinatra in concert (not entirely untrue) and whether there was any chance there might be a spare ticket. The guy in the box office, obviously impressed that someone had taken Concorde for the event, told him to come back at 5.30 that evening. Dressed smartly in a suit and looking 'the business', Steve was escorted through the hall and to a box 50ft from the stage. As the evening got under way he was joined by some people in the box next to him. Once Lionel Hampton had done the warm-up, Sinatra came on stage. After the interval, he announced that there was one of the greatest American singers in the audience. The spotlights zoomed on to the person sitting next to Steve, and Sinatra introduced Tony Bennett. 'A memorable evening', Steve recalled …

One of the events that caught the interest of the world's media was the Concorde flight on 13 July 1985 with Phil Collins aboard as part of the Live Aid concert. This monumental event, organised by Bob Geldof and Midge Ure in aid of Ethiopia's starving population, was televised around the world. Taking place at Wembley Stadium in London and JFK Stadium in Philadelphia it was described as the biggest rock concert ever, with an amazing line-up of talent. Princess Diana and Prince Charles attended the concert in London.

Phil Collins took to the stage, playing his numbers and a duet with Sting before leaving by helicopter to Heathrow where he caught the evening Concorde flight to John F. Kennedy Airport. It was reported that this was watched by 1 billion TV viewers. In a moving gesture, Concorde flew low over the stadium and as it did so dipped its wings to the roar of approval from the crowds. It was, as a stewardess friend of mine who was there said, 'a very special moment in a very special day'. When the flight landed in New York, Phil Collins was taken to Philadelphia by helicopter where he performed on stage as part of the Live Aid concert there.

THE SUPERSONIC
COMMUTERS

Of the regular commuters on Concorde no one stood out more than Fred Finn. He flew Concorde as often as we did! He knew us well, called us by our Christian names and was always very relaxed on board. He flew a remarkable 718 flights on Concorde and was named as the world's most travelled Concorde passenger, having clocked up 3 million miles, the equivalent of flying to the moon and back six times! Later, Guinness World Records awarded him the accolade of the world's most travelled man, having clocked up 15 million miles in total. Fred Finn is now president of the 'Save Concorde Group'. This team leads an enthusiastic membership aimed at getting Concorde into the skies again, albeit in a heritage capacity.

Another familiar face was David Springbett. David was a caring man who was always ready to listen to one's problems and give good advice, especially about career moves. If the cabin service had finished, he would invite you to sit down and for a few minutes we would put the world to rights. He was a great adventurer and had he been born a century or two before, I'm sure would have been one of the world's great explorers. He had huge belief that everything was achievable.

A few years previously he had set the world speed record for flying round the world and was entered in the *Guinness Book of Records*. In 1980 he had flown subsonic from Los Angeles to London, then on to Singapore via Concorde. The next stops were Bangkok, Manila, Tokyo and Honolulu, arriving back in Los Angeles on a 747. The trip had taken 44 hours and

6 minutes. He had also ensured that this trip would not cost him a penny. He had bet $500 at 20–1 that he could beat the existing record, and thereby raised enough money to cover the cost of his challenge.

A year later he beat the world record for getting from London's financial district to Wall Street, New York. Naturally this included a transatlantic flight on Concorde. With helicopters standing by at both ends, the one in London landing on a runway 20m from Concorde, he beat the record by 11 minutes, in a time of 3 hours, 59 minutes and 44 seconds. He also beat the record going from west to east.

He was yet another personality whose enthusiasm for life was infectious and it was stimulating to come across these characters on a regular basis. David kindly gave me a signed copy of the book *Skiing Down Everest* and the *Guinness Book of Records*, in which his records are documented.

Another speed record-breaker was Richard Noble. Delightfully unassuming, he was nonetheless fascinating and spoke quite humbly of his exploits. In 1983 he had helped break the world speed record in the jet-powered *Thrust 2* that reached speeds of 633.46mph in Nevada's Black Rock Desert. In 1997 he was project director of the team that built *Thrust SSC*, which was to break both the record and the sound barrier on the desert sands of Nevada with a speed of 764.03 miles an hour (Mach 1.02).

Richard also went into the aviation record books. In November 1987 he completed three Atlantic crossings on Concorde in one day (not something I would have chosen to do, even as a passenger). His new project, *Bloodhound SSC*, is the ultimate 1,000mph jet and rocket-powered car. It will be capable of achieving Mach 1.4, and is to be driven by Andy Green. This is, first and foremost, an international education initiative designed to further careers in science, technology, engineering and mathematics by showcasing these subjects in the most exciting way possible. This fascinating project will be tested in 2015 and 2016 in South Africa.

In the sporting world there were the extremes of emotion on board Concorde with the golfing elite. When the Brits brought home the Ryder Cup there were huge celebrations on board. A not-so-jubilant group were the American team after a 'drubbing' at the Belfry, recalls flying colleague Dick Bell. 'The mood on board was none too pleasant and the team proceeded to brood all the way home. Mind you,' says Dick, 'the crew were all golfers and smirking for most of the flight!'

In the Formula One motor-racing world, Bernie Ecclestone, F1 supremo, was a regular and liked to sit in seat 1A. Having known F1 team owner Frank Williams through my F1 days, it was a pleasure to meet him again on a couple of flights. He is a true gentleman and has managed extraordinarily well to lead a normal life despite the permanent injuries from his tragic accident.

Another passenger it was a pleasure to meet was none other than our boss, chairman of British Airways, Lord King. He was flying to New York with the American ambassador and he was extremely charming and approachable. A very likeable boss! He was responsible for transforming the loss-making airline into one of the most profitable in the world. In 1981, he purchased Concorde directly from the government and within a year was turning this 'white elephant' into a profit. Advertising experts were called in to change the brand image of the company and, although 23,000 jobs were shed, Lord King managed to boost staff morale when it was at a low ebb and modernise operations. Media reports suggest that the London–New York service made an annual £20 million operating profit by the early 2000s. Lord King passed away in 2005.

No chapter on the famous and regular commuters would be complete without mention of Sir David Frost. Sir David was a very regular flyer, commuting up to twenty times a year across the Atlantic and making 400 flights in twenty years. Known for his untidiness with the newspapers and his love of red wine, he was nonetheless a colourful character whom it was always a pleasure to serve. On the last ever commercial flight on which he was a guest he was asked what made Concorde special, and he summed it up beautifully by saying it had a 'friendly club atmosphere'.

If Sir Richard Attenborough was on the flight they often sat together, and if awards could be given for the most charming, affable and indeed lovable character it would have to be Sir Richard. Impeccably mannered, he was always most endearing with his 'darling' prefix when addressing us.

A very close second would be John Travolta. Known for his acting roles in *Saturday Night Fever* and, later, *Pulp Fiction*, John is an accomplished pilot, flying his own 707. He also owned three Gulfstreams and a Learjet. No doubt John enjoyed his supersonic flying experience, and despite his stardom and fame was one of the nicest and most unassuming of the A-listers.

THE 11-MILE-HIGH CLUB – THE SHORTEST CHAPTER

Undoubtedly any discussion about Concorde from those curious about the supersonic lifestyle would have to include a subtle enquiry about any shenanigans that took place in flight.

I am sorry to disappoint my readers but there was very little that went on, to my knowledge, and the lack of space was more than likely the reason. The toilets were more cramped than other aircraft and although I know of one famous American movie star who disappeared in there with his travelling companion, I doubt that whatever they got up to was very comfortable! These events were far more common on 747s due to the length of the flight, the easy access to alcohol and no doubt the boredom factor.

The elite members who joined the 11-Mile-High Club were few and far between, and they ran the gauntlet of being found out – which they invariably were. One couple who had managed to sneak into the toilet together were obviously getting carried away as the door was taking a good pounding. One of the stewards was concerned that this might disturb the passengers and informed the flight crew of these antics. There followed an announcement from the flight deck that went something like this: 'Ladies and gentlemen, we are now flying at Mach 2, twice the speed of sound and at a height of 58,000ft and for the two passengers who have just joined the 11-Mile-High Club – congratulations!'

'The male in question returned to his seat as cool as a cucumber, the female emerged with a face as pink as rhubarb,' commented my flying colleague, Bernadette. On their seat was a certificate signed by the crew. It read: 'We hope the Concorde was the climax of your trip.' Another crew member had written, 'So pleased you could come on Concorde today.'

On another occasion, a couple sitting up at the front of the aircraft were getting amorous and it was noted that they moved to the rear of the aircraft, which was pretty empty. Still puffing on his cigar the male passenger put his other hand to good use with his partner, and her moaning could be heard by the crew in the galley. The three aft cabin crew concealed behind the galley curtain peered out to see what happened next. Like the other passengers they were also handed a certificate with appropriate comments written on it. Part of our training was observation – and there was little that escaped our notice …

BREAKING RECORDS: WASHINGTON TO NICE, 11 SEPTEMBER 1984, AND A KIND-HEARTED BELLBOY

It would be fair to say that there were not many people in the world who could afford to charter Concorde in the eighties and indeed I don't know of anyone who did, apart from the trip I am about to describe. The mother of the king of one the Arab royal families had been in Los Angeles for an operation. She and her entourage had flown from Los Angeles to Washington, where it had been arranged for a Concorde to fly her to Nice.

As I was selected for this VIP trip, the schedule was to fly out to Washington, spend the night in a hotel there and the following morning to fly our guests to Nice. At a special briefing in London we were given specific instructions on how to serve food and beverages in the Arab custom – only with the left hand. No alcoholic beverages would be offered in accordance with their drinking laws. Arabic coffee and pots would also be part of the catering along with Arabic food. And finally it was compulsory to wear white gloves to 'meet and greet' the royal family.

Our Concorde flight out to Washington was very relaxed as our twelve passengers consisted of BA staff who were part of the organisational team for this exclusive charter. On our arrival at Washington Dulles Airport we were soon aware of the hospitality of our Arab hosts who had spared no expense in looking after us. We were met by three extremely long, black

In the limousine, royal Arab charter.

There were ways and means of acquiring the white gloves! Royal Arab charter.

stretch limos complete with tinted glass, TVs and a bar. There was one for the flight crew and two for the cabin crew of six (they obviously didn't want to overcrowd the mobile party room!). No sooner had we closed the doors than the sound of corks could be heard popping and glasses of champagne raised to such a pleasant day's work. It was another memorable moment to add to the long list of everyday life with the supersonic fleet.

Our accommodation for the night was a superior five-star hotel and much grander than any we normally stayed in. If this was how the rich and famous lived then I guess we were fortunate to enjoy their lifestyle for a short time. However, the euphoria of champagne and luxury soon dissipated when I unpacked my suitcase to find that my white gloves that were compulsory for this trip were missing. Since this small detail had been emphasised at the briefing and we had all nodded a positive 'yes' when asked if we had all our gloves with us, I was thrown into a mild panic.

'Where could I buy a pair of white gloves?' I asked the hotel receptionist, swallowing hard and very aware of the late hour. This would not look good on my records if, having been selected to do this exclusive charter, I turned up barehanded. The receptionist glanced at the clock. It was now six in the evening and she was sorry to tell me but all the stores would be closed by now. In another panic I phoned all the girl crew and asked if they had packed a spare pair. The replies were all negative. Then I had a flash of inspiration – had I not seen the bellboy unloading our luggage wearing white gloves?

Immediately I hotfooted it down to the lobby and, yes, there he was still wearing white gloves. But how could I persuade him to part with them? Asking nicely was my only tactic, I decided, unless I was to take him hostage in a corridor to save my own skin. The bellboy looked at me doubtfully. They were his only pair and he too needed them for his job. If anyone

The royal Arab charter – the crew at Nice Airport before flying back to London.

The certificate we received from Captain Cook on the royal Arab charter. We made history with the longest ever Concorde flight, 4,566 miles (642 subsonic) in 4 hours 7 minutes.

In Nice after the royal Arab charter.

in the immediate vicinity had overheard me pleading with the bellboy to part with his gloves I'm sure they would have been greatly amused. Finally, with the promise of a leather Concorde luggage tag, the deal was done. The gloves were removed, the tag handed over and I was saved. However, the gloves were a tad too large and that evening a lot of time was devoted to shrinking them in hot water and restoring them to an acceptable standard of white.

After a leisurely breakfast and feeling every inch superstars, we waited as the enormous black stretch limos pulled up outside the hotel to take us to the airport. The Concorde ground staff were already hard at work. Seats from the front few rows had been removed to allow more space for the royal party. The special catering, of which there was a consummate amount and enough to furnish a banquet, had to be stowed so that we knew where everything was.

When all was ready, we waited for the party who, not unexpectedly, were late. The captain no doubt had a slot of take-off times on his mind but when you charter the world's most expensive aircraft I guess it is the guests' prerogative to turn up when it suits them.

I was more than ready to display my newly acquired gloves and congratulated myself on the deal that had been brokered with the bellboy. After what seemed an interminably long time the royal party arrived. The royals, which included the mother of the king and four princes and princesses, were seated in the front section, whilst the entourage of forty-eight were seated in the rear. Suffice it to say the royal party itself was very relaxed, whilst we found the entourage the most demanding of passengers.

It was dark when we landed at Nice, but as we turned off the runway into our specially allotted parking area we were left in no doubt of the prestige of our passengers. Waiting for the doors to open and welcome the royals were a body of smartly suited minders. Behind them sat a queue of seventeen Mercedes limousines waiting to ferry the passengers to their destination.

Our working day finished at a hotel in Nice, and over drinks and a debrief Captain Cook informed us that we had made history that day. The flight from Washington to Nice was the longest recorded, a distance of 4,566 miles in 4 hours and 7 minutes, and the flight crew had signed certificates for us to record this superlative day.

The only remaining task for this charter was to reposition Concorde back to London. Captain Cook, being one of the most amiable of captains, asked us, probably tongue in cheek, what time we would like him to schedule our departure (that was definitely a first ... and last in my flying career). We all agreed that after breakfast would be perfect and so at 10 a.m. precisely we left to return the aircraft to London. The captain performed a splendid take-off and fly-past over Nice Airport. 'Just to show the French we know how to fly these aircraft', he was heard to comment.

We were soon headed back to the real world and the routine of normal flights, but not without a handsome tip for all of us from our Arab guests.

LIFE DOESN'T ALWAYS GO ACCORDING TO PLAN

There were many tales about the seating arrangements on the aircraft. One financial advisor to an Arab royal family booked a seat purely for his briefcase, which no doubt contained *slightly* more money than the cost of the fare ...

Another time, a high-ranking minister came onto the aircraft and was very insistent that he didn't want anyone to be seated next to him and asked specifically not to be interrupted during the flight to New York as he had a considerable amount of work to do. It was not unusual for many of the commuter executives to go straight to meetings after their arrival into JFK. The flying time was therefore used for work preparation, and it was not uncommon for some of them to attend their meetings and fly back to London that same day on the evening flight.

On this particular flight there was a very attractive female with long, dark hair, equally dark eyes and slim figure. She spoke with a South American accent and was extremely dressed up for the occasion. Wearing a short cream silk dress (had she just come from a party the previous night?) and jewellery that would fill a Boodles shop window, she did stand out amongst the mostly male commuter flight to New York.

Despite the lack of space in the aisles, she left her seat and strolled slowly up and down the cabin casually making note of the passengers. I watched her with interest (again, careful observation is part of our job) as it was unusual for a passenger to be so restless. When I next spotted her she was bending over talking to the minister who was supposedly hard at work. 'Is everything alright, sir?' I asked, discreetly glancing towards the South American beauty who had by now seated herself next to him.

He smiled as if he had just won the jackpot. 'Everything's fine,' he replied, looking at me guiltily.

I hoped ministers weren't in a habit of changing their minds so readily about government decisions as this one was about his seating arrangements that morning. As I served the meal to them, there were no signs of the minister's copious amounts of paperwork. The notes had been put away and the two were heavily engaged in conversation. All was obviously going well between them until, during the coffee service, one of the stewards came blustering into the galley. 'Mon Dieu!' he exclaimed. 'I have just spilt a glass of port over a lady's cream dress. Well, it wasn't my fault exactly. She knocked my hand.'

We both grabbed cloths and soda water and rushed up to where the accident had happened. This, I hasten to add, was a very rare occurrence and it would reflect badly on our standards of exemplary service. It was the pretty South American girl who, very embarrassingly, had a very large red stain in the crotch area of her dress. To our surprise she refused our help to remove it. 'Eet is okay,' she said. 'I will do it mayself.'

The steward was profusely apologetic and suggested that maybe she go into the toilets to use the soda that was very good at removing stains, he assured her. Showing not the slightest sign of distress at the ruined silk dress, she stood up and went towards the toilets in the mid-section of the aircraft. Alongside these are the crew take-off seats and a small area that can be curtained off. When I next passed, there was a very cosy, intimate picture behind the curtains of the minister kneeling with his hand halfway up her dress attempting to remove the stain with a cloth. I did wonder, as they departed the aircraft, whether it was his intention to buy her a new dress or just remove the one she was wearing in one of New York's hotel rooms …

It was very rare in all the years of Concorde service that our food made bad tabloid news. However, there was one serious incident when some of the food was contaminated with the food poisoning bug salmonella. Passengers and cabin crew were taken ill, some of them seriously. The source was traced to aspic on the canapés.

The whole episode proved to be very expensive for BA, both from a cost point of view and the public relations angle. All claims were met very generously. However, there were some who were taking no chances. Businessman Peter de Savary, who had been hospitalised after this outbreak, was in no mood to jeopardise his health on his next Concorde flight, and who could blame him? Greeting him on the flight I was handed a Fortnum & Mason's hamper to be placed in the hat rack. At the start of the meal service I guessed what was coming, but the question had to be asked – was he dining with us? He replied no and looked taken aback, as if I had just asked him if he wanted another salmonella sandwich. The hamper was removed from the hat rack and he proceeded to eat a luxurious picnic with enthusiasm.

Another story about quirky eating habits is recalled by a colleague of mine, cabin service director and cabin crew manager Dick Bell:

I remember once we had the actress Dyan Cannon as a passenger. She boarded with a large hatbox and did not want to give it up, so as the seat next to her was empty we strapped the hatbox into it. Did she want a drink? the crew asked. 'No', was the reply. Was she going to eat on the flight? Again, the answer was 'No'. After take-off she opened the lid of the hatbox and it was full to the brim with popcorn. She ate the entire contents of the box during the flight with no liquids with which to wash down the popcorn, not even water.

DO NOT UPSET THE CAPTAIN!

There is probably only one occasion where I have witnessed the captain having a difficult time with a Concorde passenger. It was an evening flight to New York and we were all anxious to get away as the weather was deteriorating. However, we had a tall American who swaggered on board and promptly lit up a cigar. Politely, I asked him to extinguish this as it was against regulations, for the simple reason that the aircraft had just been refuelled (we had about 95 tons of it around us, to be exact).

The passenger carried on smoking as if he hadn't heard a word. Getting somewhat concerned at this flagrant breach of safety I repeated my request more urgently. This was having absolutely no effect, so the cabin service director stepped in and still there was no response.

Finally the captain walked smartly down the aisle, hat on, jacket buttoned and looking every inch the commander. I have to say that he was not one of our tallest captains, rather short in fact, so when this very tall American stood up there was a considerable height difference. The American was not budging on extinguishing the cigar and one can only assume that his bravado was the result of too many pre-departure drinks in the lounge. It was a battle of wills, and to make matters even worse the American blew smoke into the captain's face. At this flagrant insouciance, the captain's face turned *rouge*. This was undoubtedly, I'm sure, the first time anyone had ever questioned his authority in uniform. It was the spark that lit the touch paper.

At the sight of two uniformed airport police approaching his seat, the American finally realised that he was in a bit of trouble. Hastily extinguishing his cigar, he was ignominiously escorted off the aircraft whilst pleading that he had to get home for an important dinner that night. Shamefully for him, he missed it and spent a night in jail before receiving a heavy fine and leaving the next day.

ALL IN A DAY'S WORK

In every strata of society there are always the prima donnas and quite unsurprisingly there was the odd one on Concorde flights. This particular lady was married to a media baron. She was indeed one of the world's lovable eccentrics.

The aircraft doors had already closed, but were hastily reopened for her late arrival. She was travelling with her son to Miami. However, it transpired that he had lost his passport and therefore had to stay behind. Our middle-aged passenger was dressed in a black taffeta mini skirt, a creased, cream, flouncy silk shirt complete with coffee stains and flat brown lace-up shoes. As she bent over in the middle of the aisle, and in full view of the passengers, she made no attempt to hide an ample display of leg covered in black tights and a crepe bandage over one knee.

Prior to the meal service, she had been drinking copious amounts of champagne interspersed with Panadol and smelling salts. On the presentation of her meal of guineafowl she immediately asked for more potatoes and added that if she didn't like the fowl she would change it for veal. The afternoon tea service was also met with a demand for more sandwiches.

On arrival in Washington, usually an hour's stopover before the sector to Miami, 'her ladyship' insisted that a message be sent to her husband to order some tranquilisers that she had left at home in London. Just as the doors were closing for departure she again insisted that another message be sent to her maid in London, as she had lost her American Express card and she thought it could be in her bed!

At this point, our normally very relaxed cabin service director came to the rear of the aircraft to tell us this story and he was, by this time, pretty wound up. Still drinking champagne, our passenger decided to order a wheelchair for her arrival, not a bad idea considering the amount of alcohol she had drunk.

We later heard from the ground staff that she had plagued them for 4 hours after her arrival. We last saw 'her ladyship' checking in for her flight to the Caribbean arguing the case against paying excess luggage. It turned out that she had twelve excess bags and this was going to cost her $80 apiece. 'But my maid packed for me,' she protested. Still, the check-in girl was unrelenting.

Then our harassed passenger tried the well-used celebrity tactic, 'Do you *know* who I am?' The calm response came that even if she were the President of the United States she would still have to pay for excess luggage. So we left her ladyship flying off to an island in the Caribbean, her son left behind in England, her American Express card somewhere amongst the bed clothes and her tranquiliser prescription somewhere in the making. Fortunately, not all our passengers had such domestic problems.

THE ROYALS AND OTHER FAMOUS FLIGHTS

In February 1977 the Queen and Prince Philip flew Concorde for the first time from Barbados to London at the end of her Silver Jubilee tour.

Then, in February 1979, they flew to Kuwait at the start of a Middle East tour. Cabin crew member Jeannette Hartley, who was on the tour, remembers it vividly. The Queen, Prince Philip and their entourage disembarked in Kuwait whilst the Concorde crew flew on to Bahrain and had four days there to await the royal party who were arriving on the Royal Yacht *Britannia*. The crew were hoping to visit the royal yacht the following afternoon but were turned away by armed guards. However, once they had explained in greater detail that they were Her Majesty's Concorde crew they were let through the gates and enjoyed a wonderful visit aboard the yacht. Other places on the tour were Riyadh and Dhahran, where the Queen met the crew and shook hands with them.

In 1985, the Queen Mother flew supersonic on her 85th birthday. This was a birthday present to her from British Airways. She was accompanied by Viscount Linley, Lady Sarah Armstrong Jones and Chairman of BA, Lord King. The Queen Mother had mentioned to Captain John Hutchinson that every time she heard Concorde coming over Clarence House she would go out onto the balcony and wave. John responded by saying that, in future, when he flew Concorde over London he would flash the aircraft headlights in salute. It became a tradition for all Concorde captains to do this thereafter.

Another royal who had flown Concorde on several occasions was HRH the Duke of York. He had a very relaxed persona. One time, on his return from Shannon, the flight was quite empty and some of the crew were taking a break and having a meal at the rear of the aircraft. Imagine their embarrassment when they saw the prince walking down the aisle as they were tucking into a steak. He quickly put them at their ease and chatted to them as casually as if they were all old friends.

A colleague of mine, Dick Bell, recounts his experiences of flying with the royals:

In 1984 I became a cabin crew fleet director and with two other colleagues managed all of the Concorde cabin crew. Along with my day-to-day duties I was also given the responsibility of managing flights for the royal family and the prime minister of the day and any other special flights such as air shows and Ryder Cup flights. These flights were planned down to the finest detail. Wherever you went you knew there would be thousands of people watching your arrival, such was the appeal of the aircraft, so everything had to be just right. It really was a flying superstar.

To fly in formation with the Red Arrows was fantastic but not as nerve-racking as the first time I was involved in the arrangement and operating of a royal flight for Her Majesty the Queen. Many other royal flights followed, but the first is always the one you remember the most. It was a twelve-day tour of the United States and, like the Queen Mother, the Queen is a joy to look after and to be around. She puts you at ease the first time you meet her.

The crew underwent several briefings during the build-up to the flight, usually starting a month before. The Air Commodore of the Royal Flight was in charge of the itinerary and the crew worked closely with him on protocol matters. His advice was to 'be natural'. The briefings included everything from the Queen's likes and dislikes, to menu choices and protocol, and how she liked her drinks. Two favourite drinks of Her Majesty are a very dry Martini and a gin and Italian vermouth, the old 'gin and it', as we knew it. The only difference is that Her Majesty likes it two-thirds gin and one-third Italian, instead of the other way round (nice, I tried it). Prince Philip had a preference for Watney's Red Barrel that, somehow, was still available.

Because these flights were regarded as private flights there were no announcements and no safety demonstrations. Her Majesty made herself at home and had photographs of the family around her in the cabin that was furnished with a dining table and two chairs. She is a small eater and, although I have mentioned her favourite drinks, her consumption of alcohol was minimal.

The 1991 US tour included stops at Washington, Miami, Tampa and Austin, Houston and Kentucky. The Queen travelled with her entourage including her surgeon, ladies-in-waiting, a butler, maids and hairdresser and many others. During the flight, the Queen would invite prominent members of her entourage – maybe her surgeon and the foreign minister – to dine with her. It was interesting to note that the age-old royal protocol still firmly applies that when the Queen finishes eating, so does everyone else around the table.

An interesting part of any royal flight takes place after landing. Before landing, the Queen's dressers (she has two) laid out on her bed the outfit she was to wear on arrival along with the jewellery, gloves, hat and handbag. As soon as the aircraft pulled off the runway and whilst taxiing, the Queen went into her 'bedroom' to change, so when she emerged from the aircraft she had only been wearing the outfit for no more than 2 minutes. And the aircraft had to arrive exactly on time – to the minute.

One incident I will always remember happened just prior to landing in Washington. The Queen was finishing her lunch and she knocked a glass of red wine directly into her handbag, which was beside her on the floor. I took away the handbag and cleaned it up.

On another occasion on a 767 flight to South Africa the aircraft landed to a very windy day. The doors were opened and as the Queen stepped out in her somewhat large hat she saw the press standing behind the barriers waiting to photograph her. Behind clenched teeth and looking directly ahead she commented, 'I think this is the wrong hat!'

Being the consummate professional that she is, she managed to battle with the wind and keep her hat firmly in place.

Julia van den Bosch recalls her experiences of royal flights where the ladies-in-waiting had to change in the toilet, not an easy task in such a confined space, whilst the accompanying male members changed into their ceremonial dress in the cabin. During the tours to the USA they landed at air force bases and not the hugely organised commercial airports. Here, there were no catering trucks driving up alongside to replace the used cutlery and plates. Julia recalls that whilst they were lavishly entertained at embassy parties on the tour they still had the job of washing up in the small galley sink, a far cry from the glamour of the tour they were on.

Flying colleague Sue Drayton hosted Princess Diana on Concorde to the annual Council of Design awards at the Lincoln Center in 1986. (Princess Diana, at that time, had dramatically changed hairstyle to having it gelled back for the occasion.) Sue recalls that her amazing navy dress hung on the back of the flight deck door and Sue was most concerned that it didn't arrive smelling of food from the galley, which was just behind the entrance to the flight deck.

Another of the concerns when royals are flying is that the toilets are always kept pristine, and checks are made constantly. However, just before landing it was not unknown for excess rubbish to be bagged up and stored in the toilet for landing. Sue had just done this when Princess Diana made a last-minute visit to the toilet. On opening the door and seeing the confined space loaded up with rubbish bags, she smiled at Sue saying, 'Sorry, a girl's gotta do what a girl's gotta to do', and waited patiently whilst Sue hastily and, no doubt somewhat embarrassed, removed the offending bags.

CREW SHENANIGANS: YOU WOULD EXPECT IT, WOULDN'T YOU?

The flight crew were always good fun to be with as they loved their job and were always enthusiastic about their work. There were twenty-four captains and the same number of co-pilots and flight engineers. Some had an interesting history. For instance, one had won the King's Cup Air Race, another had been the UK aerobatic champion and another as a young fleet air arm pilot had been involved in a mission to sink the *Torrey Canyon*, a tanker that had run aground on the Cornish coast in 1967. Suffice it to say, he missed his target and his first drop incinerated the cliff top! This became a bit of a joke amongst the flying crew. In fact, on one Concorde flight the first officer calmly announced that the captain flying the aircraft had been assigned to bomb the *Torrey Canyon* and missed. There was nervous sniggering amongst the passengers …

It was inevitable that members of a small select fleet leading a pretty exclusive lifestyle and enjoying nights away in romantic places would form close friendships. It happened on long-haul flights. It also happened on Concorde.

Sometimes these 'friendships' developed into something more, and inevitably relationships were sometimes formed between the flight crew and stewardesses. The flight crew also had a bid line so it was simple to arrange flying with a woman of their choice! There was the heady cocktail of attractive, single (and sometimes not so single) females and the silver braid of the flight crew flying a prestigious plane and, hey bingo, it's a mix as lethal as a cigarette and a tanker of fuel. We all knew who was seeing whom. Some made little secret of the fact. If a couple did manage to keep their relationship low profile, it didn't last very long. Everyone who knew went about their own business and passed little comment, and they did not play 'judge and jury' at what went on.

I do recall one amusing evening, but perhaps not so amusing for the couples involved. British Airways held a reception for Concorde flight crew and cabin crew and their wives and partners at the Concorde Centre at Heathrow Airport. I remember it well as I arrived on crutches having just torn my knee ligaments on a skiing holiday. However, I'm sure the pain in my knee was mild in comparison to the discomfort of some of the flight crew who arrived with their wives.

It was very unusual for any of us to come face to face with the 'anonymous spouses'. I think it was generally a case of 'out of sight, out of mind' for some of the crew. And I don't remember many incidences where the pilots took their wives away on trips with them – for the simple reason that the New York trips were so short, it was hardly worth all the effort of flying 3,500 miles for one night on the town.

So, at this party there was a highly charged atmosphere of girlfriends mingling together, while avoiding their flying 'other halves'. It really was a case of keeping an eye on who was in the room and sidestepping around any would-be hazard in the form of a wife. Because of this, the atmosphere was quite strained and I did wonder how many present actually enjoyed the evening.

THE CONCORDE CRASH

One of the questions I am most frequently asked when Concorde comes up in conversation is why did the world's only supersonic aircraft have to stop flying and was it the Air France Concorde Paris air crash that sealed its fate?

On 25 July 2000 the unimaginable happened. An Air France Concorde with a full complement of 100 passengers and nine crew took off from Charles de Gaulle Airport. As flight AF4590 gathered speed down the runway and lifted into the air, the controllers in the control tower, who had just given the aircraft clearance for take-off, were horrified to see flames pouring from its left-hand side wing. They wasted no time in informing the captain (the flight crew would have been unable to see the catastrophic fire that was about to change the destiny of that flight and all those aboard).

At less than 200ft, the aircraft reared up, its damaged wing now engulfed in fire. It dipped to one side and fell back to earth. The doomed aircraft had made just 90 seconds of its flight. The captain's intention had been to take it to Le Bourget Airport, a few kilometres away. As it was, the aircraft could not make that distance and came down in the suburb of Gonesse, hitting a small hotel and killing four people and all passengers and crew. The intensity of the fire was so great that the first firefighters on the scene could not approach the crash site.

Flight AF4590 had been carrying German tourists, including three children, bound for New York. The passengers were to join a cruise to Ecuador, South America, via the Panama Canal. It was to have been a holiday of a lifetime.

The Concorde experience had not started well for them. The aircraft had been delayed by 2 hours after it was found that there was a problem with Number 2 engine and its reverse thrust. The captain had waited until the fault had been rectified. Captain Marty was 54 years of age and had 317 hours of experience on the aircraft. He was a daredevil skier and had gained fame by windsurfing across the Atlantic some years before.

The problem fixed, the passengers boarded the aircraft, excitement mounting now that they were finally on their way to enjoy the supersonic experience to New York. However, as the Concorde gathered speed down the runway, a fire started and a sequence of events unfolded that made this incredibly safe and beautiful aircraft doomed to a tragic end.

How had the fire started? One of our senior and most likeable Concorde captains, John Hutchinson, flew Concorde for fifteen years. He is an aviation consultant, speaker and broadcaster and his views are much respected in the airline industry. In 1999 he was installed as Master of the Guild of Air Pilots and Navigators. He commented on the accident (I quote), 'the fire on its own should have been eminently survivable, the pilot should have been able to fly his way out of trouble'. Captain Hutchinson believes that there were a number of factors – a combination of operational error by the flight crew and 'negligence' by the Air France maintenance department that led to the crash.

A Continental Airlines DC10 bound for Houston had taken off minutes earlier, losing a 44cm piece of metal from its undercarriage. It was lying on the runway and in the path of Concorde flight AF4590 about to take off. As the fully loaded Concorde gathered speed it hit the metal strip with such force that it caused one of its tyres to burst. Even though Concorde tyres had been developed to withstand impact they had not been designed to withstand hitting such a large piece of metal at such speed.

With the impact of the tyre bursting, a large piece of rubber from one of the tyres flew up and with the force of a missile hit the fuel tank. The fuel tanks were so full that the impact of the rubber hitting the tank caused a shock wave that had nowhere to dissipate, causing it to rupture. Fuel escaped from the hole and ignited by a spark, probably from an electrical wire. There was now a dramatic fire situation.

Captain Marty and his crew were at that time beyond the point of return. They were committed to take off. The vivid images we have are of a rooster tail fireball spewing out from the Number 2 engine and Concorde's final moments before it plunged back to earth.

One of the disturbing facts that came out of the accident report was that as the aircraft gathered speed, it was skewing down the runway towards the grass verge. As a result it hit a yellow landing light that disintegrated into engine Number 1, thereby causing it to fail. It would appear that Captain Marty had no choice but to take to the air. The aircraft was about to leave the runway and at that speed there would have been a major incident and fire on its own.

To add to the potential of a further catastrophe, the Concorde would have been heading straight towards a 747 that had just landed from Japan and was waiting to cross the runway from which the Concorde was taking off. On this aircraft were President Jacques Chirac and the First Lady of France, returning from a G7 summit in Tokyo. It would have been a 'no choice' decision. If the captain of the Concorde had continued off the runway and onto the grass there would have been a cataclysmic accident and many, many fatalities – and France could have lost its president.

The take-off speed of flight AF4590 was 188 knots, 11 knots below the minimum recommended speed. Under normal circumstances the captain still had enough speed to climb away, but no longer enough power. Number 1 engine had failed and Number 2 engine had been shut down by the flight engineer because of the fire. This was at a crucial time when the remaining thrust from that engine was vital for its survival. But what had caused the aircraft to yaw to the left as it sped along the runway?

This remains a controversial subject. Two leading Air France Concorde pilots prepared a sixty-page report of the crash which they submitted to the investigating judge. They maintain it was the nose wheel that had been improperly repaired causing the skewing motion. A week before the crash, the doomed aircraft had been in the hangar for maintenance. With both the British Airways and Air France Concordes, they were subject to strict procedures of inspection. Various load-bearing components such as the undercarriage bogeys had to be replaced at regular intervals and after a few hundred flying hours.

The stress on the wheels is more than any other aircraft, the reason being that the delta shape wings provide hardly any lift on the ground. On Concorde's take-off, lift is achieved when the captain pulls up the nose and pitches the aircraft to an angle of 11 degrees. Up until then the wheels and bogeys bear the full 185 tons of Concorde weight.

In the case of the doomed Concorde, it left the hangar missing a spacer. This is a 304.8mm-long and 127mm-diameter piece of anodised aluminium – a vital component of the landing gear that keeps the wheels in alignment. Although it had flown to New York twice in that time, the condition deteriorated to the extent that when flight AF4590 lined up on the runway there was nothing to keep the front wheels in line with the back. It was similar to a supermarket trolley that veers to one side if the wheels are not aligned properly.

The BEA (French accident investigation bureau) maintain that the aircraft's yaw to one side was not caused by the missing spacer but by the fact that the aircraft had lost the power of both engines on the left side. However, the Concorde captains disagree. In the training simulator they are trained to experience an engine loss shortly before take-off. In John Hutchinson's words, 'It's no big deal at all. The yaw is totally containable.'

For a few agonising seconds after take-off the captain got the aircraft up to 210 knots, only for Number 1 engine, which had begun to recover, to fail again. But what makes this story even more cataclysmic in its unfolding is the other factors that came to light after the investigation.

It wasn't only mechanical errors that led to the crash. The aircraft was overweight. When the captain lined up on the runway his instruments would have showed him that he had 1.2 tons of extra fuel on board. This should have been burnt off during the taxi. Further, there were nineteen extra bags that were not included in the manifest (the aircraft's documentation). These had been loaded at the last minute and weighed another 500kg. This brought the aircraft to within an estimated 6 tons of its allowable weight given the wind conditions at the time.

In the interval between the Concorde leaving the terminal and reaching the runway, another circumstance occurred. When the flight left the terminal there was no wind. In between leaving the stand and reaching the take-off point the wind had increased to 8 knots, but it was a tailwind. An aircraft will always take off *into* the wind, the reason being that this gives it extra lift. John Hutchinson comments, 'The captain should have insisted on taxiing back to the other end of the runway, as most Concorde pilots have done in the past, and taken off into the wind. It appeared that the captain and his crew did not react to this information at all.' They failed to respond to the fact that the aircraft was now several tons overweight and beyond its aft centre of gravity limit, given the conditions. A senior industry source stated that, 'Even in a take-off with all four engines working normally you are well beyond the point where the test pilot has been prepared to tread.'

Another factor in the fate of this flight was that had the aircraft not been overweight, it would have been airborne before it hit the metal strip that caused the fire, and the experts say the captain would have got away with it. But, according to Captain Hutchinson, his options were severely compromised and the captain found himself, 'trying to save a one-time thoroughbred which was responding like a flying pancake'.

In the concluding chapter of this tragic unfolding of events, flight AF4590's fate was sealed with one final act – 25ft off the ground, the ailing Number 2 engine which had ingested some of the runway light was shut down by the flight engineer. This breached the set procedures that require that no engine is shut down until the flight is stable at 400ft, and then only on a set of commands from the captain. The flight was doomed, and the great white bird so graceful in flight fell to an untimely and horrific end, along with its precious cargo of passengers.

The crash was a horrifying reminder that Concorde was not the invincible piece of supersonic machinery that we had all assumed after its twenty-four years. For myself and other crew members, the image of that crash remains as indelible as any other heart-wrenching events of our generation, ranking alongside such historical moments as the assassination of John F. Kennedy and the collapse of the New York Twin Towers on 11 September 2001. It was impossible to comprehend.

THE AFTERMATH

After the disaster, ironically enough BA did not ground their Concorde fleet. Normal flights were resumed the following day, much to the anger of the Air France Concorde management, who believed that all the Concordes should have been grounded after such a disaster. It was three weeks later on 15 August that an announcement was issued informing that the certificate of airworthiness for the fleet was to be withdrawn. At the time, a British Airways Concorde was taxiing onto the runway bound for New York. It was ordered to return to the stand and all flights were suspended.

Although Concorde had the highest safety record of any commercial airliner, like any long-serving aircraft faults were beginning to appear. In 1989, fourteen years before it came out of service, defects were beginning to manifest themselves. An American commentator and author, William F. Buckley Jnr, had chartered Concorde for a round-the-world trip in a bid to beat the speed record. With 100 Americans on board, the rudder, a 9ft piece of tail, disintegrated whilst flying at 40,000ft. The captain was unaware of this until the control tower at Sydney International Airport noticed a sizeable chunk missing from the Concorde's tail.

Despite Concorde's reputation as being the best maintained aircraft in the world, this did little to reassure some of the American passengers who flew home from Sydney by sub-sonic means. It must have been a huge shock to the flight crew to emerge from the front door of the aircraft and look down the fuselage to find the huge gap where the rudder had been.

During a period of thirteen years Concorde suffered another four problems with its rudder sections falling off. Moves were made to strengthen their design. Failing rudder sections were not the only incidents. There were another three in six weeks on one occasion. On a flight to New York, a Concorde had to return to London after an engine was shut down. Later, three aircraft windows shattered as cracks were found in one of the outer layers of the one of the windows.

The irony of these incidents was that, after the Paris crash in 2000, the remaining British Airways and Air France Concordes were given a £30 million refit. The fuel tanks were strengthened and made safer with Kevlar, designed to be bulletproof. The tyres were also strengthened. An internal refurbishment was carried out by Sir Terence Conran and designer Adam White at a cost of millions of pounds. Thirteen months after the Air France crash, the British Airways fleet had their certificate of airworthiness restored. Concorde was ready to take to the skies again and loyal Concorde passengers were royally entertained by the Chairman of BA with caviar and champagne in one of the hangars. BA was desperate to woo them back to their favourite aircraft.

Before the scheduled services were put into action, Captain Mike Bannister had arranged to fly Concorde halfway across the Atlantic as a familiarisation for the pilots, crew and ground staff. On its return, everything having gone so well, the pilots, the cabin crew and all those involved in Concorde's re-entry into service were very upbeat. Concorde was to be restored to her natural place in the skies again.

However, on their return to London they were met with devastating news. An aircraft had flown into one of the Twin Towers in New York. Further news came through that another plane had deliberately crashed into the second tower. All at British Airways knew what this meant for Concorde. In the 9/11 disaster Concorde lost forty of its most frequent commuters – bankers, executives and heads of industry. Concorde's revenue would be hugely hit.

But the writing was already on the wall for the supersonic era. Despite its good safety record, and it was the best maintained aircraft out of any other fleet, management were deliberating its future. Air France, having had another incident with one of its aircraft, was also deliberating whether to keep its Concordes in service. Bookings were down and these were sadly exacerbated after the disaster of 9/11.

British Airways also had to accept the economic realities of the Concorde operation. Passenger numbers were falling, yet the fuel costs for supersonic flying were astronomical. During the grounding of the Concorde after the Air France crash it was also noted that the airlines made more money flying their first-class passengers subsonically than on the fuel-guzzling Concorde.

Another factor was Airbus. The aircraft's manufacturer had detailed discussions with British Airways confirming the need for an enhanced maintenance programme in the coming years. Maintenance charges would go up by £40 million. British Airways decided that such a huge investment could not be justified at a time when there was a global downturn in all forms of premium travel and, more relevantly, on Concorde.

Prolonging Concorde's life was becoming a losing battle and, as BA pointed out, by the year 2009 Concorde would be 40 years old. Concorde, however, never made its 40th birthday. It was to retire after twenty-seven years of commercial operations. In the case of Concorde, age was purely relative. As a BA spokesman was quick to point out, the aircraft did fewer landings and take-offs than any other fleet. It was in the air for considerably less time than the subsonic aircraft, and was therefore in much better shape.

But the few problems that occurred attracted more attention from the press, for the sole reason that it was such a high-profile aircraft, and it was to survive barely two years after the Paris crash. However, despite the 9/11 disaster, services resumed in November 2001.

Two years later the crowds were gathering at Heathrow to watch its final exit from the skies. After the last flight had landed at Heathrow and the press, the TV crews and public had disbanded after what had been a momentous day, the poignancy of the event was recalled by Chief Pilot Mike Bannister, who had flown the last commercial flight in from New York a few hours earlier. As he left the hangar he recalls it was a misty night, and on the tarmac neon lights were shining on five perfectly serviceable Concordes that he knew would never fly commercially again. It must have been a heart-wrenching moment.

British Airways now had the dilemma of what to do with these iconic aircraft. It was decided that they should be shared around the globe. In October 2003 G-BOAC flew to Manchester, where it is now a fixture at the Runway Visitor Park. This was followed five days later by G-BOAG, which flew to Seattle via New York to the Museum of Flight. The final resting place for G-BOAD was New York and the Intrepid Sea Air Space Museum. Concorde G-BOAA, which never flew again after the grounding in 2000, is at the National Museum of Flight in Scotland and G-BOAB, retired in 2000, now resides somewhere at Heathrow Airport.

A popular destination for Concorde during the winter months was Barbados. Alongside Barbados' Grantley Adams Airport is a hangar that now houses Concorde G-BOAE. Here, visitors can enjoy the 'Concorde Experience' and even try a flight simulator.

At Brooklands Museum in Surrey is the production aircraft G-BBDG that was used extensively in the test programme in the early seventies. On 13 February 1974 it was first flown by Peter Baker and Brian Trubshaw from Filton to Fairford, and it was the first aircraft to carry 100 passengers at Mach 2.

At Duxford Imperial War Museum is the pre-production Concorde (GAXDN) that was used for testing.

The final flight ever of a Concorde took place on the historic day of 26 November 2003 when Concorde G-BOAF took off for Filton, near Bristol. It was no coincidence that in 1969 the first British Concorde had taken off from here. The public was again out in vast numbers – 1,000 spectators watched her fly from Heathrow. The sight of crowds lining the Clifton Suspension Bridge as she passed over will remain etched on my memory as I watched it on TV.

At Filton, amongst the 20,000 crowd to see G-BOAF land, was HRH the Duke of York, who received Concorde's last flight log from Chief Pilot Mike Bannister. His words gave a fitting end to the Concorde chapter when he described Concorde in his speech as the 'icon of the century'.

On board this flight were crew members Louise Brown and Julia van den Bosch, who between them had over fifty years' supersonic flying experience. Louise recalls the poignancy of taking leave of the aircraft for the final time. Both she and Julia were very subdued. Louise got off first. She left Julia, the longest ever serving Concorde stewardess, to say her own personal goodbyes to the ghosts of the past and the aircraft to which she had devoted twenty-seven years of her career.

AND FINALLY …

Concorde has been hailed many times as the greatest engineering achievement of the twentieth century and there will not be many who would wish to contradict this statement. In every way Concorde was way ahead of its time when its design and development began in the sixties.

It left us with a wonderful legacy that, although at the time of its inception appeared to be a massive drain on the country's finances, gave the British public an icon to be proud of. It gave the future generation a hope that our small nation can still be a world leader in new technology. Although only a small number of the population ever flew on the British Airways Concorde (over 2 million), those who did will never forget the experience. So many times I have listened to someone's account of their flight on Concorde. Their eyes light up, their voice becomes animated and they recall every detail indelibly embedded in their memories. Then their ebullience fades as they mourn its demise.

And one final story about our beloved aircraft, as told by Captain Jock Lowe. It is as amusing as it is revealing of Concorde's prowess:

American spy planes had been sitting over Cuba for years. The pilots of these aircraft were at 60,000ft and sitting in spacesuits. One day the spy plane was asked to move 30 miles north as an airliner was passing. And there went Concorde … 100 passengers in shirt sleeves drinking vintage champagne.

The Future of Supersonic Flying

So what is the answer to the question so many Concorde fans would like to know? What are the chances of Concorde ever flying again? Ex-operations manager at Brooklands Museum, Jan Knott, who was in charge of Concorde charters for twenty years, has this to say: 'There's no one in the world who'd love to see that happen more than I would. But the costs of getting it up and running again would just be phenomenal.'

British Airways removed any chance of its reappearance into the skies, even in a heritage role, when it disabled its electrical and hydraulic systems and, according to one expert, to reinstate these would cost hundreds of millions of pounds. Air France Concorde enthusiasts are keeping their options open and hoping to maintain the engines in an airworthy condition. However, the Save Concorde Group, of which there are 3,000 members and with Fred Finn as president, is still holding on to the belief that it can be done in a heritage role.

And as for the future of supersonic transport? The buzz word is *hypersonic* travel and speeds of up to Mach 6 at 250,000ft – London to New York in 1 hour, London to Tokyo in 2 hours … and the development of a spy plane that has neither the beauty nor elegance of Concorde. Pictures of this American spy plane, Aurora, came to light when mysterious loud bangs were heard the length and breadth of Great Britain and in New York in December 2014. A theory was put forward that Aurora was flying across the Atlantic!

Again, the cost and design issues of developing something similar into a passenger plane are being mooted as astronomical. And so, whilst we send missions to Mars and find out more about our universe with techniques that scientists could only dream about several decades ago, we have no immediate replacement for supersonic travel – and probably not in my lifetime.

Concorde will be confined to the history books and supersonic passenger travel will be a part of it too. For now …

Concorde at the Intrepid Museum of New York. (Courtesy of Frederic Carmel, freeimages.com)

POSTSCRIPT:
CROSSING THE ATLANTIC –
3 HOURS AND 30 MINUTES
TO SEVENTEEN DAYS

Flying across the Atlantic on Concorde on a regular basis brought home to me how technology in such a short time had shrunk the world. Three and a half thousand miles of ocean was reduced in time to a mere lunch service. The early explorers could have had no comprehension that one day man would achieve this. It was as hypothetical as putting a man on the moon.

The time between the first powered aeroplane by brothers Wilbur and Orville Wright in 1903 and the rolling out of the first prototype Concorde from a Toulouse hangar was a mere sixty-four years. It was a remarkable achievement in the time-scale of history.

Having flown across the Atlantic many times in a subsonic aircraft in a time of 7 hours 30 minutes and crossed it the fastest possible way, supersonically, it occurred to me that to experience the full enormity of what Concorde could achieve, it was only right that this ocean should be crossed by slower methods.

In 1996 my family and I booked a cabin on the *QE2* and made the crossing in four and a half days. This was not without incident. Once out in the Atlantic we experienced the full force of a gale and it was interesting to watch the height of the waves as we sat enjoying dinner in an almost deserted restaurant. Cabin portholes were sealed off and we were not allowed up on deck to take a breath of air with a 60mph wind ready to whisk us off the decks as the ship ploughed on towards Newfoundland. As we approached the coast we ran into a blanket of fog and were diverted around the Long Island crash site of the TWA 747 that had gone down a few weeks earlier. Speculation was rife, even then, that it had either been a terrorist attack or an accident by the American Navy during missile practise.

During this eventful voyage, and in between perusing the five-course menus and wave watching from the comfort of the ship, it set me wondering about what it would be like sailing in those massive breaking waves on a small yacht. From the safety of the massive tonnage of the *QE2*, it seemed inconceivable that a yacht could survive in that vast boiling morass of breaking foam – and so another challenge was born.

Two years later I had signed up to do an Atlantic crossing on an 80ft round-the-world Whitbread yacht called *Creightons Naturally*. Exactly how old and tired this boat was and its standard of seaworthiness was only made clear to me when we set out from Las Palmas in the Canaries bound for St Lucia. Three hundred miles into the Atlantic Ocean, life aboard was full of drama. Having left the calms of the Canary Islands we headed into strong winds. We all had to take a turn at helming and this was not easy in the cross-beam breaking waves. It took a considerable amount of concentration.

In one day we managed to damage two spinnakers (the large curved sail at the front), destroy one large grinder on deck (a hefty steel rounded instrument for 'grinding' in the sails) and the glass cover for the instrument panel. The cabin below was a chaotic mess of a spinnaker graveyard and a chandler's workshop.

Aside from crewing duties we all had to take turns at preparing meals. The galley was small and antiquated and cooking three meals a day for eighteen people was not easy when the yacht was being tossed around by the Atlantic swells. It made Concorde's Atlantic crossing seem extremely civilised in comparison. To add to our galley duty day we were also assigned to cleaning the floors and heads (toilets) after finishing the cooking duties.

Four days into the trip we were allowed our first outdoor shower using sea water, with a quick hosing off with a litre of fresh water. It felt wonderful. Over the next few days we had problems with the rigging and almost keelhauled a spinnaker after the spinnaker halyard (the rope that holds the spinnaker up to the top of the mast) snapped. One of the crew climbed the mast to retrieve it and found another of the mast's support ropes had frayed. Racing was now abandoned as crucially we had to sail, or rather nurse, the boat across the Atlantic to prevent the mast falling down. All this drama, and 1,400 miles to the nearest landfall.

During that time the wind dropped, the Atlantic swell lessened to a more or less flat pond and we were becalmed. Boredom now became an issue. Luckily, a yacht on its way to Barbados passed close by. It was motoring and diverted course to come and see us. Seizing the opportunity to relieve the tedium, our male crew dressed up as pirates and swam the 100 yards to 'board' the Finnish boat and drink vodka with its crew. We also gave them some fuel from our well-stocked tanks. This small interlude greatly enhanced the routine of wind watching and listening to the sound of sails lurching idly in the 'doldrums'. The girls on the crew also took a dip in the Atlantic. It made us feel very insignificant when one stopped to consider the vast ocean below and around us.

By this time we were drinking putrid-tasting water that was rationed. We did not have the luxury of a water maker that other transatlantic yachts took with them by way of necessity. We had also finished the last green vegetable in the form of tinned peas. I developed a sympathy with the sailors of old who grew sick and went down with scurvy. Would we be in similar condition when we arrived in St Lucia? At least those sailors had enjoyed a daily rum ration – that was not on our ship's agenda!

On day ten the navigator shouted to everyone, 'We've only got 1,000 miles to go!' Now, for someone like myself who had only cruised the Solent or done a sprint across 90 miles of the North Sea, this sounded like a lot of miles, but we were by now on the homeward leg.

By day seventeen we spotted landfall. This was a defining moment in the trip. I was roused from my bunk wearing only a T-shirt and underwear and was promptly handed the helm by the skipper. After weeks of seeing nothing but ocean this dot of land became the focus of our attention. This was one of my most exhilarating moments of the trip as I helmed the boat towards our destination which, until now, had been an unseen island existing only on the chart plotter. My state of undress was only a minor matter.

As the island of St Lucia grew larger we revelled in our achievement. We had finally made it across that large ocean despite all the challenges that nature had thrown at us. We had experienced a tropical storm with a deluge of non-stop rain lasting 24 hours, complete with a water spout, wild seas, flat calms and beautiful sunsets and nights lit by a million stars.

We had also shared many ridiculously funny moments. Even during the many crises when we lost faith in the seaworthiness of the yacht we had bonded together. Someone amongst the crew had always managed to find the funny side of things and bring a smile to our faces. During the crossing we had spotted flying fish, dolphins and a spouting whale. The joy of being so close to nature and the ocean was something one could never ever experience flying on a supersonic jet across the Atlantic.

LIFE AFTER CONCORDE

The supersonic crews are now part of a small elite club consigned to history. The beautiful aircraft we worked on are now sadly sitting idly in museums. Whatever the future holds for supersonic flying, we all have wonderful memories and I hope this book will give an insight into the lifestyles of the Concorde crews for Concorde lovers to enjoy.

What did we do after we left British Airways? Obviously there are too many to mention here, but here are a few of my old friends:

Jeannette Hartley is a guide at Brooklands on Concorde.

Julia van den Bosh leads a very busy life as a textile designer and exhibits nationally.

Louise Brown lives in the Cotswolds and works part time as an estate agent.

Bernadette Forrest is now married and still leads an enviable life travelling to exotic holiday destinations.

Jill Channon is married to Mike Channon, the racehorse trainer.

Scarlett Geen is married to a wine importer and is a very keen tennis player.

Several of the BA Concorde captains, including Mike Bannister, John Hutchinson, Brian Walpole and Jock Lowe, are sought after as guest speakers at various society dinners and functions, as well as giving lectures aboard cruise ships.

And finally myself? I am a very keen sailor living by the coast, and a member of three yacht clubs. I also work as a yachting photographer: visit my website at www.solentpics.com. When I'm not enjoying myself on the water, I have found time to pen several novels.

Concorde profile. (Shutterstock, Image ID: 2922877. Copyright: Kevin)

CONCORDE TIMELINE

1959: Government committee recommends that the UK builds a supersonic passenger jet.

29 November 1962: Anglo-French treaty signed. A wide range of airlines begin to make non-binding orders.

2 March 1969: First flight.

1 October 1969: First supersonic flight.

21 January 1976: Concorde enters service with BA300, flying from Heathrow to Bahrain.

24 May 1976: Concorde flies to Washington DC.

22 November 1977: Concorde starts flying to New York, JFK.

27 March 1984: Concorde begins flights to Miami via Washington.

13 July 1985: Phil Collins performs in both Live Aid concerts in London and Philadelphia, courtesy of Concorde.

25 July 2000: Air France Concorde crashes outside Paris with 113 killed.

15 August 2000: BA flight to New York returns to gate when cause of Paris crash emerges. Concorde grounded.

11 September 2001: First post-crash proving flight with passengers lands at Heathrow just after the attacks on the World Trade Center.

10 April 2003: BA and Air France announce the end of Concorde.

24 October 2003: Concorde's last passenger flight, BA 002 New York to Heathrow.

26 November 2003: Last flight, to Filton.

CONCORDE'S VITAL STATISTICS

LENGTH: 203ft 9in (62.1m)
WING SPAN: 83ft 8in (25.5m)
FUSILAGE WIDTH: 9ft 6in (2.9m)
HEIGHT: 37ft 1in (11.3m)
INTERNAL HEIGHT: 6ft 5in (1.96m)
FUEL CAPACITY: 26,286 imperial gallons (119,500 litres)
RANGE: 4,143 miles (6,667km)
TAKE-OFF SPEED: 250mph (400km/h)
CRUISING SPEED: Mach 2 (1,350mph/2,160km/h) up to
    60,000ft (18,288m)
LANDING SPEED: 187mph (300km/h)

If you enjoyed this book, you may also be interested in…

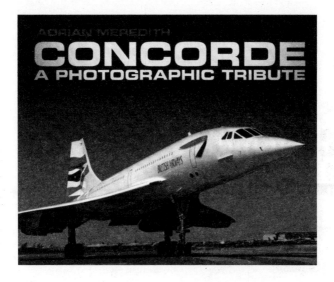

Concorde: A Photographic Tribute

ADRIAN MEREDITH

Concorde can surely claim to be the world's favourite aircraft. Its sleek lines and glamorous design made it an icon recognised all over the world. Travelling at twice the speed of sound at 60,000ft, to fly Concorde was the dream of many and the regular pastime of the lucky few. The rich and famous graced its all-first-class cabins, some time and again; Sir David Frost notably undertook around twenty flights a year on Concorde for an average of twenty years. Photographer Adrian Meredith spent many years photographing Concorde from every conceivable angle. Here he has collated his artwork to present a full-colour account of this remarkable and memorable aircraft. Including information and photos from behind the scenes as well as significant milestones and detail on the passengers and personalities on board, this is a unique and beautiful photographic tribute. In this new and updated edition, ten years after Concorde's momentous last flight, Meredith looks at the potential of supersonic and hypersonic travel with fascinating speculations and images of what the future holds.

978 0 7524 9324 4

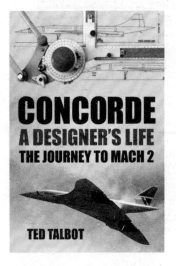

Concorde: A Designer's Life

TED TALBOT

Much has been written about Concorde itself, but little about the people who designed it. This book is part autobiography that encompasses some of the team, several technicalities and a good measure of the lighter side of the job. Ted Talbot, who began his career at BAC as an aerodynamicist and became chief design engineer, has combined the technical narrative with personal reminiscences to remind us that engineers have lives too. The path to Mach 2 was bumpy, with threats of cancellation and much international opposition, but this generally indicated to the Concorde team that they were on the right path!

978 0 7524 8928 5

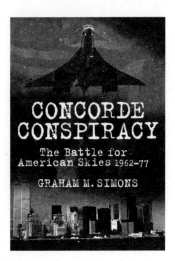

Concorde Conspiracy

GRAHAM M. SIMONS

An innovation in aviation development, Concorde was the subject of political rivalry, deceit and treachery from its very inception. This is the story of ten years of behind-the-scenes political intrigue, making use of inside information from two American presidents and the FAA, as well as declassified papers from the CIA and President Kennedy on how the Americans planned to destroy Concorde and their own American SST. *Concorde Conspiracy* is a must read for any enthusiast on supersonic flight and anyone who enjoys a real-life conspiracy.

978 0 7524 6365 0